Pratt of the *Argus*

A play

by Michael Birch
adapted from the novel by David Nobbs

Samuel French — London
New York - Toronto - Hollywood

PRATT OF THE ARGUS

First performed at the West Yorkshire Playhouse on 12th
October 1991 with the following cast:

Susie Baxter
Andrew Dunn
Jackie Lye
Paul Rider
Willie Ross
Paul Slack

Directed by Jude Kelly
Designed by Saul Radomsky
Lighting by Jenny Cane
Sound by Mic Pool
Assistant Director: Vicky Featherstone

CHARACTERS
(in order of appearance)

Henry, a junior reporter
Cousin Hilda, his severe, caring relative
Barry Frost, her amateur musical lodger
Doreen Frost, the amateur musical lodger's wife
Tommy Marsden, Henry's famous footballing friend
Helen Cornish, a flirtatious journalist
Neil Mallet, a resentful journalist
Ted Plunkett, Helen's fiancé, also a journalist
Denzil Ackermann, an arts and show business journalist
Terry Skipton, a bad-tempered news editor
Colin Edgeley, a pugnacious journalist
Ginny Fenwick, a war/fashion journalist
Ben Watkinson, a sports journalist
Norman Pettifer, Hilda's cheesy lodger
Mr O'Reilly, her reticent lodger
Mr Redrobe, a disappointed Editor
Lorna Arrow, Henry's childhood country girlfriend
Lady Behind the Counter, Henry's prurient interrogator
Uncle Teddy, Henry's shady uncle
Derek Parsonage, Henry's shady uncle's shady associate
Lampo Davey, an arty, old public school chum of Henry's
Mrs Hargreaves, the Hampstead mother of another old
    public school chum
Diana Hargreaves, Henry's teenage town girlfriend
Paul Hargreaves, an old public school chum of Henry's
Mr Hargreaves, Paul's father, a surgeon
Roger, Barry Frost's amateur Stage Manager
Bill Holliday, a local gangster/scrap dealer
Auntie Doris, Henry's Auntie with airs
A Côte D'Azur Cutie, a French dancer from Kent
A Côte D'Azur Cutie, a second French dancer from Kent
A Côte D'Azur Cutie, a third French dancer from Kent
A Côte D'Azur Cutie, a fourth French dancer from Kent
Sergeant Botney, a brutal army sergeant
George Timpley, a tragic tobacconist
Rev. Peter Hazard, the celebrant of Auntie Doris's
    second marriage

Geoffrey Porringer, Auntie Doris's lover with blackheads
Fred Hathersage, a property developer
Eric Lugg, Lorna Arrow's fiancé
An Army Officer, a wet Territorial Army officer
Brian Furnace, Henry's National Service friend
Hilary Lewthwaite, Henry's complicated fiancée
Anna Matheson, his uncomplicated girlfriend
Italian Waiter, a helpful waiter in Siena
Mrs C. E. Jenkinson, Henry's dead father's pub landlady
Cllr Lewthwaite, Hilary's fallen father
Sam Lewthwaite, Hilary's horrible younger brother
Angela Groyne, Bill Holliday's gangster's moll
Arnold Nutley, a stuntman/hitman lorry driver
A Film Director, a brush with film-making
French Waiter, a helpful waiter in Cap Ferrat

The play takes place in Yorkshire, London, northern Italy,
and southern France

Time —1956 to 1957

DOUBLING

One actor plays Henry, the other parts are played by two female and three male actors, or by a cast of forty nine.

Casting breakdown for six actors

Henry

Cousin Hilda, Helen Cornish, Lorna Arrow, Mrs Hargreaves, a Côte D'Azur Cutie, Hilary Lewthwaite, Mrs C. E. Jenkinson, Angela Groyne

Doreen Frost, Ginny Fenwick, Lady Behind Counter, Diana Hargreaves, Auntie Doris, a Côte D'Azur Cutie, Anna Matheson

Terry Skipton, Ben Watkinson, Norman Pettifer, Derek Parsonage, Mr Hargreaves, Bill Holliday, Sergeant Botney, Geoffrey Porringer, Fred Hathersage, an Italian Waiter, a French Waiter

Ted Plunkett, Denzil Ackermann, Colin Edgeley, Mr O'Reilly, Paul Hargreaves, Roger, Uncle Teddy, a Côte D'Azur Cutie, Brian Furnace, Cllr. Lewthwaite, Arnold Nutley, a Film Director

Barry Frost, Tommy Marsden, Neil Mallet, Mr Redrobe, Lampo Davey, a Côte D'Azur Cutie, George Timpley, Rev. Peter Hazard, Eric Lugg, an Army Officer, Sam Lewthwaite

SYNOPSIS OF SCENES

ACT I

ACT II

AUTHOR'S NOTE

Sound

Between the scenes a taped sound collage should be played which sets the time and the period. Obviously there is much recorded popular music which, with a little research, can be reasonably assumed to belong to 1956 and 1957. What is not so well known is that there are several published collections of political speeches, news broadcasts, current events and sporting achievements, produced mainly by the BBC, which are available from major retailers.

In choosing the music and the news items, it could be entertaining to contrast Henry's personality with the overt sexuality and confidence expressed in early rock-and-roll. The more serious aspect of the story, his internal and individual struggle for truth and integrity, could benefit from the irony of being put alongside the Suez crisis, duplicity on a grand scale and the final gasp of the British Empire.

Michael Birch

ACT I

Scene 1

The Midland Railway Station, Thurmarsh, near Sheffield. January 1956

Popular music and radio news extracts play

The Lights come up

Cousin Hilda, of a certain age, is waiting

A train is heard arriving

Henry, podgy, enters with a suitcase. He stands, not seeing Hilda

Pause

Hilda I see army hasn't knocked daydreaming out o' thee.
Henry Cousin Hilda! It's good to see you.

Hilda sniffs

   Thank you for coming to meet me.
Hilda Ee, Henry Pratt, duty's not beholden.
Henry I was thinking about the time I came home from the countryside after
   the war. My dad was standing on this platform. He only had one eye.

Hilda sniffs

Hilda Water under t'bridge. Let's get home for us tea.

   *Doreen Frost, late thirties, enters with luggage. She is followed by Barry
   Frost. They both have Midlands accents*

Doreen Desist, Barry! It's no use.
Barry Doreen, don't be unreasonable.
Doreen It's me or Rawlaston Amateur Operatic, Barry. You choose! Me or
   The Desert Song!

Doreen exits, followed by Barry

Hilda Ee, in front of whole world on t'Midland Station! I am contaminated by association!

Henry Do you know them?

Hilda My left room on t'front was a haven for that man when she threw his belongings out t'window!

Henry Pardon?

Hilda He's one of my gentleman lodgers! A plannin' officer from t'Town Hall w'personal problems. I took him in out of the goodness of my heart and here I am shamed in a station. Well, they originated from Walsall.

Henry (*taking out a notebook; writing*) "Council Planning Officer In Platform Musical Marriage Mayhem."

Hilda If it's not shame it's disappointment — couldn't tha have chosen a proper job? Journalism! (*She sniffs*) If tha poor parents were alive they'd turn in their graves.

Henry I want to expose injustice and search for the truth.

There is a slight pause

Hilda We'd better get home and get us tea first then.

Tommy Marsden enters. He is brisk and young

Henry Hey up, where's fire, young Tommy?

Tommy By the heck, Henry Pratt!

Henry Cousin Hilda, this is Tommy Marsden, star player with United. We were at school together.

Tommy Escaped from army, 'ave tha?

Henry Oh aye, National Service. Bloody horrible, met some good oppos though. To think thee and me were in t'same gang together.

Tommy Ee, Paradise Lane gang.

Henry I'm going to work on t'local paper.

Tommy Tha's not?

Henry I am. Tommy, is tha married or owt?

Tommy Chuff me, no! Manager says many a promising career's been nipped in bud because a player's shagging himself to death.

Hilda has an apoplexy

I'm off to London, I'm on t'transfer list.

Henry We must have a jar, sup some lotion.

Tommy Oh aye.

Tommy exits

Henry He hates me. (*He calls after Tommy*) That were a cracker you scored against Oldham! (*He makes notes*) "Shagged-Out United Star Deserts Home Team."

Hilda All them thees, thas and t's, Henry? Fancy speakin' t'that lad in t'common way?

Henry Was I, Cousin Hilda?

Hilda Tha knows right well. Tha's bin educated to better things, Henry Pratt.

Henry Better things, of course. Right, what's for tea?

Hilda ⎱ (*together*) Brawn.
Henry ⎰

Henry My dad hated brawn. He was another wreck in uniform, poor old sod.

Doreen enters followed by Barry

Doreen I'm not staying in that house on my own, Barry.

Barry You threw me out.

Doreen Details! I can't bear pernickety men.

Barry (*to Hilda*) Hang on, I'll give you a lift. Is this Henry?

Doreen Next train, Barry. My mother's very understanding.

Barry I'll move back in.

Doreen You and the female chorus, I suppose.

Doreen exits followed by Barry

Hilda It'd be sinful to spend good money for t'bus even if he is cause for comment.

Henry You must be perished waiting.

Hilda This coat'll stand some weather. (*She quickly straightens Henry's clothes. She sniffs*) I've decided sommat. I've decided to hand on to you my alarm clock. Don't be surprised to see it sitting on t'dressing table. It's got an extra loud bell. I thought tha'd be used to loud noises after t'army.

Henry Thank you, Cousin Hilda. It'll be very useful.

Hilda (*sniffing*) Mrs Wedderburn'll be glad tha's back. I met her in t'Co-op yesterday. I won't use Lipton's no more. I don't like my Mr Pettifer's cheese counter, it's no use pretending I do.

Henry How is Mrs Wedderburn?

Hilda Worse than she lets on. That woman's a martyr to her legs. She said straight out, "Hasn't your Henry turned out well?"

Henry Mrs Wedderburn makes me sound like a cake.

Hilda I've booked us a bracing fortnight at Bridlington to bridge the gap, before tha starts tha new job. Look happy, Henry, it's a surprise.

Barry enters

Barry Doreen has boarded the train to Walsall. Our marriage is over. Can you cope with Hilda on your knee, Henry?
Hilda What!
Henry "Spinster Suffers Heart-Attack in Front Seat Knee-Trembler."

The Lights cross-fade to:

SCENE 2

The newsroom of the "Thurmarsh Evening Argus"

Popular music and radio news extracts play as the scene changes

There are desks, typewriters, and phones. Henry, Helen, Neil and Ted are at work. Terry Skipton, the news editor, is in charge

Helen (*pert, fair, and not shy*) I know about you. I like to keep abreast.
Henry Do you? I mean, hallo. I mean, thank you.
Neil (*deep in research*) How d'you do. Speak in a mo.
Helen Henry Pratt, Neil Mallet.
Neil Thank you, Helen.
Helen Neil is "Thurmarshian", he's dying to tell you. "The Thurmarshian" weekly opinion column.
Ted (*a man of the world in his own eyes*) Do you have any good contacts, Henry?
Henry What?
Ted People you know whom you can use to get stories off. Obviously not since you don't know what it means.

Ted exits

Helen Ted writes the Kiddies Club column. The little dears are the Argusnauts, and do good deeds, and Ted is Uncle Jason. You'll get to know us all better this evening. We foregather in *The Pigeon and Two Cushions* at the end of the day.
Henry *The Pigeon and Two Cushions*?
Helen Opposite. You know, journalists, lawyers, policemen and criminals drink there. I may sit next to you if you're lucky.
Henry I can't be late for me tea.
Helen Sorry?
Henry I haven't got any work to do.
Helen Bluff.

Helen's phone rings. She answers it

   (*Into the phone*) Morning. *Evening Argus.* (*She turns aside and continues her conversation unheard*)

Denzil enters. He is wearily immaculate

Denzil Ah, a fresh face. A really fresh face. One of those strange faces that ought to seem repellent but which one finds oddly attractive because one doesn't find them repellent.
Helen Denzil's outrageous.
Denzil Denzil Ackermann, arts and show-business and walking cliché. I can tell you loathe me. You'll get over it. Neil, a new young friend for you.

   Denzil exits

Terry Mr Pratt. Good-morning.
Henry Ah. Yes.
Terry Keen to prove yourself, are you, Mr Pratt?
Henry Very much.
Terry Well, appearances can be deceptive.
Henry Pardon?
Terry I said you don't look promising.

Terry's phone rings. He answers it

   (*Into the phone*) Good-morning. *Evening Argus.* (*He continues his conversation unheard during the following*)
Helen Don't mind him, he's only as bad as he looks.
Henry He looks terrifying.
Helen Nobody is kind to the just not very attractive. If he was the Hunchback of Notre Dame he'd be the life and soul of the party.
Henry I feel like I'm back at school.
Helen A news editor's only pleasure in life is to despise reporters.
Terry Mr Mallet, is Thurmarshian going to welcome the onrush of sophisticated nightlife to our northern industrial town or is he going to condemn it, as a potential outrage to modern decency?
Neil Pardon, Mr Skipton?
Terry They've given the go-ahead for a nightclub in the town. Do you require assistance in lifting the telephonic instrument, Mr Mallet?

Neil picks up the phone and makes an unheard call during the following

Helen A nightclub in Thurmarsh! Ooo Henry!

Colin enters. He has large biceps in his own mind

Colin Another low dive for the Thurmarsh underworld to hang out in.

Helen Henry, Colin Edgely, our fearless criminal reporter.

Neil Bit of a professional dilemma, Helen; am I for the nightclub or am I against it?

Colin Say it's an outrage. Much more exciting.

Helen (*to Henry*) You don't have integrity, do you, Henry?

Henry Oh yes. But I try not to bore people.

Neil Is that an insult?

Helen I hope so. (*To Henry*) You're obviously a very passionate person.

Terry Mr Pratt, I am aware, of course, that your conversation is much more important than anything a mere news editor might have to say but if you could drag yourself away from Miss Cornish for a tiny moment. A man's phoned in about a cat. Pop in on your calls and see if you can make something of it.

Henry Yes, Mr Skipton. Of course, Mr … (*To Helen*) What calls?

Helen You have to make regular calls to the general hospital, the infirmary, the central police station, the Gaswork Road police station, that sort of thing. In search of stories. It's the main part of your job.

Henry Nobody told me.

Helen You're expected to know.

Terry Oh, Mr Pratt. Many's the journalistic ambition that's been pickled in alcohol.

Henry Pardon?

Terry You're welcome.

A phone rings. Henry picks it up

Henry (*into the phone*) Evening, Morning Argus. I mean …

Terry groans

The Lights cross-fade to:

SCENE 3

The back bar of "The Pigeon and Two Cushions"

Popular music and radio news extracts play as the scene changes

Henry is looking at "The Evening Argus" and sitting next to Ginny, who is rather big

Henry Three lines at the bottom of page eight.
Ginny I didn't set the world alight on my first day either.
Henry My other piece about the cat didn't make it.
Ginny It will, they use everything in the end.

Henry stares at his story

Stop thinking about it. (*She pauses slightly*) Do you have any brothers or sisters, Henry?
Henry No. I'm an only child.
Ginny What about family?
Henry My mother was knocked down by a bus and my father hanged himself in the outside lavatory.
Ginny I'm sorry.
Henry Why? It wasn't your fault. I was brought up by an uncle and aunt, Uncle Teddy and Auntie Doris. Only he got sent to prison, er, Rangoon.
Ginny Rangoon?
Henry For four years with remission. Then I went to live with this other relative, Cousin Hilda. I'm staying with her again, temporarily.

Neil enters

Neil I didn't set the world alight on my first day either, Henry. But look at me now, half the West Riding hangs on my words.
Ginny Neil Mallet, judges in black caps who've just read your virulent prose are the only people who hang on your words.
Neil Ginny is intense, Henry.

Ben, a grizzled sports correspondent, enters, with Helen

Ben Name the four football league sides that have an "X" in their names?
Helen Hallo, Ginny.
Henry Exeter.
Helen Room for a little one.
Neil There's space here, Helen.

Helen inserts herself next to Henry

Henry Wrexham. Halifax.
Helen You've met Ginny, have you, Henry? She's our fashion correspondent who wants to be a war correspondent.
Ginny I'm allowed to have ambitions.
Helen Crewe Alexandra.

Neil Well done.

Denzil enters. He puts a drink down in front of Henry

Henry Thank you, Denzil.
Denzil Dear boy, your first six o'clock gathering in the back bar of *The Pigeon and Two Cushions*! Tell me which artists do you like best?
Ginny You don't have to play, Henry.
Henry Oh, I'm fine, Ginny. Um, Impressionists. Definitely.
Denzil Really?
Ben Name all the British teams that have "Athletic" in their name.
Helen Oh, Ben. You don't have to play, Henry.
Henry Charlton.
Denzil I don't know him.
Henry Charlton Athletic. Constable.
Neil Mr Redrobe — our great and good editor, Henry — is fully behind a firmly moderate view of British morals *vis-à-vis* the nightclub.
Ginny We don't want to know, Neil.
Ben You must have meant Dunstable. I think they're Dunstable Town, anyway.
Henry Alloa.
Denzil You're pulling some obscure ones out of the hat. Basque, is he? He sounds Basque.
Henry Klimt.
Ben Not including foreign teams.
Henry Gainsborough.
Ben I think they're "Town" as well, and I didn't include non-league.
Denzil You like Gainsborough?
Neil I'll just go home and do my laundry.

Neil exits

Henry I couldn't think of anybody else.
Helen Oh Henry.
Henry Rembrandt. Bournemouth and Boscombe. Botticelli. Hamilton.
Helen They're Academicals.
Henry You must be keen on football, Helen? Not that I'm surprised or anything.
Ginny Then why comment?
Helen I support Stockport County.
Henry I'm a Thurmarsh United fan, myself. I know Tommy Marsden.
Denzil I've done my duty. Good-night children everywhere. See you in Fleet Street. Ouch, did I touch a nerve?

Denzil exits

Ginny Denzil's outrageous.

Helen You know Tommy Marden?

Henry We were at school together. We were in the same gang. The Paradise Lane Gang. Named after the street where I was born.

Helen Then you do have a contact.

Ginny Careful, Ben will get jealous.

Ben Happy-go-lucky's my middle name. Welcome to the madhouse. Ben Watkinson. Sports Correspondent. Got to go home now and give the wife one.

Ben exits

Ginny Time I was off as well. I've got to review the Splutt Players production of *Candida*.

Ginny exits

Helen Come home with me, Henry.

Henry I've got to get back for me tea.

Ted enters and puts a drink in front of Henry

Ted Never mind, Henry Pratt, I didn't set the world alight on my first day either.

Henry Thank you. You're all very welcoming.

Ted Day one of your future career. What's the verdict?

Henry A bit … you know — but very stimulating.

Ted The qualities of a good journalist are pretty hard to define but on first sight I'd say your qualities were — pretty hard to define. One thing I will say, you seem to be getting on very well with my fiancée.

Henry chokes, spitting his beer voluminously

I'll just pay a call, Helen, and we'll be off to the Shanghai Chinese Restaurant and Coffee Bar. I don't suppose you'll want to join us, will you, Henry?

Henry I've got to get back for me tea.

Ted exits

Helen A gorgeous woman just offered you her body.
Henry Did she? I mean, I only started in the heady world of newspapers this
   morning. Anyway I've got a girlfriend, we met long before I went into the
   army. You were joking?
Helen Will you ever know?

Neil enters

Isn't your laundry waiting urgently, Neil Mallet?
Neil My brother from the print room was in the other bar. Do you know, our
   intrepid crime-reporter, Colin, is only eavesdropping on Bill Holliday in
   there, as obvious as a private eye in a "B" feature film!
Helen Bill Holliday's a scrap dealer with a murky past, Henry.
Neil You aren't really going to marry Ted, are you?

Ted enters

Ted Isn't your laundry waiting urgently, Neil Mallet?
Helen Good-night, Neil. (*She winks at Henry*)

Ted and Helen exit

Neil (*looking at the paper*) "What the stars wear next to their skin?" by Helen
   Cornish. What d'you reckon to our Helen, eh Henry?
Henry Helen means nothing to me. I'm spending a night of bliss with my
   gorgeous childhood sweetheart from the countryside in the Midland Hotel
   on Friday.

Colin enters, rushing

Colin Oh God! Act normal.
Neil I will!
Henry I am!
Colin He might come through.
Henry Who?
Neil When?
Colin Bill Holliday and right now. It was my evidence sent two of his best
   cronies down for a suspended sentence and he's never forgiven me!
Henry What?
Colin He's got a knife!
Neil You mean ... ?
Henry A knife!
Colin Believe me.

Henry Why?

Colin He said "Why?" Either you've got nerves of steel, or you're a pratt, Henry Pratt. I'm telling you that man's a bonfire of hatred! And I could be the spark.

Neil Oh God.

Colin Just a few sharpened coins. Better than knuckle dusters.

Henry D'you mean … ?

Colin But you'll be all right with me, kid.

Henry I've done nothing.

Colin Anyone I'm seen talking to's implicated.

Neil I've got to do my laundry.

Neil exits

Colin Don't show him you're nervous! He's got eyes where other people have ears. Time for another at *The Globe and Artichoke*, kid?

Henry I've got to get back for me tea.

The Lights cross-fade to:

SCENE 4

Cousin Hilda's basement living-room

Popular music and radio news extracts play as the scene changes

Mr Norman Pettifer, Mr Barry Frost, Mr O'Reilly and Cousin Hilda herself are relaxing, if that is the right word. The small television is switched on. Barry is learning his lines, and humming the lead from "The Desert Song"

Norman We had an amazing run on Wensleydale today. Last week it were dull. Cheddar, Cheddar, Cheddar. It's discouraging when you pride yourself on the widest selection in the West Riding and all you're asked for is Cheddar.

There is a slight pause

Mr O'Reilly Oh yes.

Hilda Mr Pettifer, tha knows tha mustn't get Mr O'Reilly excited, it's bad for his asthma.

Norman Sorry. We did have an amazing run on Wensleydale.

Barry An amazing run, how amazing.

Norman Do I detect sarcasm at all, Barry Frost?

Hilda turns the television off

Barry Don't turn it off on my account.
Hilda It's late. We've had Alma Cogan. All we've got now is some people looking at paintings and talking, and a lot of Austrians yodelling on their zithers. Anyroad, it's common to keep the television on when you're having a conversation.
Mr O'Reilly Oh yes.
Barry (*singing*) "Bring me some men, who are stout-hearted men ..."

Hilda sniffs

Norman Call it instinct if you like but I have a strong suspicion that tomorrow is going to be a Red Leicester day.

Henry enters, very ill

Hilda What sort of a time d'you call this? Tea's in t'oven. Gravy'll be congealed but tha'll just have to lump it.

Henry heaves

Henry I think I've bin sick on t'stairs.
Hilda Oh!
Henry I know I was sick on t'lawn.
Hilda Oh!
Henry I was sick all over t'coal as well.
Hilda Oh!
Norman He's been drinking.
Henry Ee, Norman Pettifer! How's the cheese counter? (*He winks at Hilda, then heaves again*)
Norman You can't upset me by insulting cheese.

During the following, every mention of cheese increases Henry's agonies

I'm proud of cheese. In fact my life is like a runny Camembert. My personality could be likened to the runniest of runny Camemberts. It wouldn't hurt me even if tha said I smelt like a powerful Gongonzola. I'll make you a nice cup of sweet tea.

Henry collapses in a chair

Norman exits

Hilda I've failed you, Henry. I've failed tha poor dead parents. That alarm clock sitting up there totally unappreciated.
Henry Shurrup!

Hilda runs from the room

(*Producing the current "Argus" from about his person*) Bottom o'page eight. At Dalton Public School — did you know I went to public school, for two years? It's a long story … Mr O'Reilly knows.
Mr O'Reilly Oh yes.
Henry At Dalton I was famous as, "Henry ee-by-gum-I-am-daft Pratt". Bottom o'page eight.
Barry Unless you wrote this advert for adding two inches to your height with undetectable shoe lifts, I require more co-ordinates.
Henry I'm allowed to have ambitions, so don't mock.

Norman enters with a mug which he gives to Henry

(*Drinking*) This sweet tea's black coffee with no sugar.
Norman I mentioned sugar deliberately to make you feel ill. I can be a right bugger.
Henry You read my story. Second column. Foot o't'page.

Barry passes the paper to Norman

Hilda enters

Hilda The stairs are passable. Journalists!
Norman (*looking at the article*) What's "thives"?
Barry "Thives"?
Henry The first printed word of Henry Pratt.
Norman "Thives, who last night broke into the Blurton Road home of Mrs Emily Wetherald, seventy-three, stole a coat, a colander, and a jam jar containing five pounds in threepenny bits."
Barry His first story.

The newspaper is given to Hilda

Henry A misprint in my first word in print. Is it an omen?
Norman Did you make a good impression?
Henry Mr Redrobe, our great and good editor, believes in chucking you in at the deep end.

Norman It's the same with cheese.

Henry Cousin Hilda, now I'm working, I want to pay you a proper rent.

Hilda Rent!

Henry I don't want to be indebted.

Hilda Indebted! You are not one of my lodgers, Henry Pratt, you are my son.
Well, you are now. You're my responsibility.

Henry I don't want to be a responsibility. I'm not ready for the responsibility
of being a responsibility.

Hilda If I took rent from tha, tha'd be on a footing with Mr Pettifer!

Norman Pardon?

Hilda Or Mr Frost.

Barry I'm temporary.

Mr O'Reilly I'm permanent.

Hilda Coming in here, drunk, offering me rent, disturbing Mr O'Reilly. I
don't suppose tha'd offer rent to our Doris and her fancy man. Or happen
tha'd rather live wi'them in their pub in t'country?

Henry I don't want to live with Auntie Doris. I want to live here.

Barry (*singing*) "And pigs might fly …"

Henry There's another thing. I've got to go to London at the weekend.

Hilda London! Tha told me tha was staying over wi' Malcolm Hammond
on Friday night.

Henry Malcolm Hammond on Friday night … ? (*He remembers to lie*) Oh
… I am, I haven't seen him for ages. No, on Saturday morning. I'm going
to see a rugby match.

Mr O'Reilly Oh, rugby.

Hilda Ten minutes to cocoa, Mr O'Reilly. You see, Henry Pratt, the
consequences of self-indulgence. Mr O'Reilly's getting excited. Couldn't
even fit in a bit of a trip to Bridlington but tha can go gallivantin' off to
London. (*She sniffs*) Anyroad it wouldn't be the same. The floral clock's
flooded.

Henry snorts with the effort of subduing his laughter

I'd hoped t'army would teach thee respect; it seems I'm doomed to
disappointment. Is tha rehearsin' up t'scratch, Mr Frost?

Norman It's on the end of next week.

Barry Any sarcasm there, Norman?

Norman You're probably nervous. It's just the same with ——

Barry If you compare *The Desert Song* to cheese I'll shove this cup right up
your arse!

Hilda Mr Frost!

Henry "Planning Officer in Spode Backside Horror". This argument's my
fault.

Hilda No, it isn't.

Henry I'm sorry about everything I've ever done.

Hilda Stop being so big-headed. Henry has transgressed, which is plain for all to see; still, his father were a drunk.

Henry Shurrup!

Hilda bites her lip, mortified

Hilda Right, conversation. Money, sex, food, drink, pleasure, religion, politics are all contrary to t'rules of the house. Anything else, I've no objection.

Mr O'Reilly I was t'inkin'. If the Almighty had meant us to play rugby he'd have given us oval balls, isn't that right?

Henry, Norman and Barry collapse with amazed laughter; Hilda is mystified

The Lights cross-fade to:

SCENE 5

The Editor's neat office at the "Evening Argus"

Popular music and radio news extracts play as the scene changes

Mr Redrobe, the neat Editor, faces the subdued Colin and Henry over his desk

Henry Good-morning, Mr Redrobe.

Colin Good-morning, Mr Redrobe.

Mr Redrobe Shut up, Mr Edgeley. (*He picks up a letter*) You were bodily ejected from *The Globe and Artichoke* by the landlady after causing significant damage to a variety of fixtures and fittings.

Henry I'm sorry, Mr Redrobe.

Mr Redrobe We pride ourselves on having a good relationship with the licensed trade.

Colin High spirits, nothing more; the landlady used a completely inappropriate level of violence.

Mr Redrobe Shut up, Mr Edgeley. (*He picks up a second letter*) You stole a red light, got arrested and gave your name as Groucho Marx.

Henry I'm very sorry, sir.

Mr Redrobe We pride ourselves on having a good relationship with the police force.

Henry My behaviour fell very short of my own high standards, Mr Redrobe.

Colin And so did mine, sir.

Mr Redrobe Shut up, Mr Edgeley. (*He picks up a third letter*) Your substitute parent asks if you are likely to be sick all over her house every day so she can make plans to replace the stair carpet with lino strips.

Henry She was upset because I didn't go home for my tea.

Mr Redrobe We pride ourselves on having a good relationship with our staff's families.

Colin I always vomit discreetly.

Mr Redrobe Shut up, Mr Edgeley. Your excuse is you were excited by spending an evening with members of my editorial staff?

Henry Yes, sir.

Mr Redrobe Good God.

Henry I wish to offer my humble apologies, sir.

Mr Redrobe Journalism, Mr Pratt, Thurmarsh style, is rather pedestrian. The "high standards" which you so spectacularly fell short of would be no doubt a godsend to us all in the event of a story of national or international moment coming your way. But since you are more likely to report on the painting of a new hopscotch grid in the local playground I think a more modest and workmanlike approach would better become a junior provincial journalist.

Henry Yes, sir. Is mine going to be the shortest newspaper career on record, sir?

Mr Redrobe I shall put the blame entirely where it belongs. On Mr Edgeley. Who is to take this as a severe warning.

Colin Thank you, Mr Redrobe. I'll see he doesn't disgrace us again.

Mr Redrobe Mr Edgeley, there are some people who are journalists because they possess an enquiring mind and are burning with a driving need to comment on the world around them, there are others who are journalists because they are idiots. Mr Pratt, English education fails dismally to fit people for real life; I gather you performed a rather all-embracing tour of the system?

Henry Urban elementary, followed by country local, back to urban elementary, then state grammar, then private preparatory, followed by public boarding, finishing back at state grammar.

Mr Redrobe You're a total mess, Mr Pratt.

The Lights cross-fade to:

SCENE 6

The Rundle Café

Popular music and radio news extracts play as the scene changes

Grease and steam. "Children's Favourites" with Uncle Mac full blast on the radio; Max Bygraves sings "I'm a Pink Toothbrush"

There is A Lady Behind The Counter. Henry is with Lorna

Henry Could it be a bit quieter?
Lady Tha knows what tha can do if tha doesn't like it.
Henry But it's for children.
Lady Customers like it at a decent volume.
Lorna I love children. I wanted to have your children.
Henry Lorna, you will.
Lorna No, I won't. A room in the Midland Hotel! It were a washout. Last night were a complete waste of your money.
Henry It wasn't all my fault.
Lorna You upset me. You were ashamed of me in front of your friends.
Henry Lorna Arrow!
Lorna Yes, you were! I told them I was a waitress in pub in the country and you blushed purple. I'm your dark, guilty secret from the past. You want me to be interesting and keen on books and paintings and ideas and foreign countries and things, and I'm not.
Henry I only want that you should want to reject the role that society wants to put you in.
Lorna I don't want to be a film critic.
Henry Who's talking about film critics?
Lorna Imagine me ordering sweet cider with me pamplemouse in Hampstead.
Henry Who's talking about Hampstead?
Lorna The railway station's round the corner from this café, isn't it? You're going to London right now, aren't you?
Henry To see an England rugby international.
Lorna To see Diana Hargreaves. Or have you forgotten posh Diana Hargreaves now you're working with the fabulous Helen Cornish? She's a cow, that one.
Henry Lorna, she's not.
Lorna You've been flirting with her.
Henry Of course I haven't.
Lorna Then why are you so embarrassed?

Henry She's more sophisticated than I'm used to.

Lorna And I've got nits in my hair and dangle a bit of straw out my mouth.

Henry (*to the Lady*) Please! That song could drive me to breaking point! (*To Lorna*) How are you getting on with my Auntie Doris?

Lorna She's quite friendly.

Henry It's a good job, then?

Lorna Except for her horrible man. He keeps touching me up. He rubs up against me behind the bar when Doris isn't looking. How do folk get to be so disgusting?

Henry That's awful. Nobody rubs up against my Lorna.

Lorna I'm not your Lorna.

Henry You are. I love you, Lorna.

Lorna You don't.

Henry I'd been looking forward to spending the night with you for two years!

Lorna I've lost you, Henry. We've lost each other.

Lorna exits

Teddy and Derek enter

Teddy Two teas.

Henry (*to the Lady Behind the Counter*) Last night was a night of passion; I was disappointing.

Lady 'Ere, you can't speak to me like that!

Henry Will you turn it down, please?

Lady I'll tell your mother.

Henry You'll have to dig her up then. She's been dead ten years.

Derek Something wet and warm, eh, Teddy?

Lady (*to Henry*) Don't say such things to me!

Henry Uncle Teddy!

Derek I only said "something wet and warm".

Teddy Good God, it's Henry!

Lady Are you related to this dirty young ugly mug?

Henry Hallo, Uncle Teddy.

Lady He's just told me he's had a night of passion.

Derek Ah, the advantages of youth.

Lady Ugh, you filthy old man.

Derek You've never met me!

Lady Wi' relations like you, no wonder lad's a degenerate.

Teddy He doesn't know this young man from Adam.

Lady Some people bring nudity into everything!

Henry Teddy, I haven't seen you since I was fifteen.

Derek Is this boy something to do with you, Ted?

Henry I'm his son, aren't I, Uncle Teddy?

Lady Oh, it's all coming out now.

Teddy Henry, this is a business colleague, Derek Parsonage.

Derek (*shaking hands with Henry*) Do you often have nights of passion?

Lady (*shocked again; to Teddy*) Tha's lad's father, gi'him a beltin'.

Teddy I have no children.

Lady Pull the other one.

Teddy (*to Derek*) Doris and me were never blessed.

Henry For your information, madam …

Lady Call me "madam" and you'll get this dishcloth in your face.

Henry I was only going to say that my one-eyed father hanged himself in the outside lavvie in protest at the injustice of post-war industrial Britain.

Lady He's a communist.

Henry It's the end of me first week on the *Argus*, Uncle Teddy.

Lady A communist journalist.

Henry Would you believe Helen Cornish, a reporter, asked me to go to bed with her?

Lady A sex-mad communist journalist.

Henry I refused on account of my true love, Lorna, but my true love has just walked out on me, so now I wish I hadn't refused.

Derek What a life he leads.

Henry Auntie Doris — (*to the Lady*) that's his separated wife — (*back to Teddy*) is not happy with her new man in my opinion. I was just thinking about her.

Teddy Thanks, Henry.

Derek Are you going to enlighten us as to how this altercation began?

Henry Uncle Teddy sent me to public school so as I'd be out of the way so that he and Auntie Doris could have holidays in Cap Ferrat …

Teddy Derek meant with the lady behind the counter.

Henry Oh. The volume.

Teddy I'd love to hear all your news sometime, Henry.

Henry You must. After all, you're virtually my … When my dad died Uncle Teddy took me in as his son, Mr Parsonage. His house, *Cap Ferrat*, named after their holiday hideaway, became my home. Not his fault he went to prison ——

Teddy Henry!

Henry Rangoon.

Derek Fancy you two running into each other here.

Henry Coincidence or fate? D'you know one of the chaps I used to fag for at public school is playing for England, and I'll be sitting next to Diana Hargreaves at Twickenham Rugby ground this afternoon. She's the sister of someone else I went to public school with.

Lady Ee, tha heartless Casanova! What about Lorna? What about Helen?
Derek Where could you take Helen for a little wining and dining, my boy?
Teddy We're opening a nightclub.
Derek Lightening the grey skies of Thurmarsh with a touch of Mediterranean colour.
Henry You'll need contacts. I'll be making contacts.
Teddy What d'you think of him, Derek? Will he make a man of the world?
Derek If it runs in the blood, Ted.
Henry Is this club going to be shady? There's no danger of you taking another trip to Rangoon again, is there?
Teddy Don't you have a deadline or a train to catch, boy?
Henry Uncle Teddy, I haven't seen you for over five years!
Derek Nice chat.

Teddy and Derek exit. The Lady Behind the Counter turns the radio off

Lady Some people don't deserve Max Bygraves.

The Lights cross-fade to:

SCENE 7

The stands at the Twickenham Rugby Ground. A cold winter's day

Popular music and radio news extracts play as the scene changes

Seated are Mr Hargreaves, Mrs Hargreaves, Diana Hargreaves, Paul Hargreaves, Lampo Davey and Henry. They are watching a match with thousands of others. They are equipped with rugs over their knees, a vacuum flask and a full picnic — unlike most of the others

Lampo Please God let them change ends or suck lemons soon!
Henry Why did you come, Lampo? You hate sport.
Lampo Tosser and I have barely human nature in common, but I did share a study with him for two years. Besides I'm addicted to occasions.
Henry Oh, Tosser! Did you see that?
Mrs Hargreaves Henry, you do appreciate French food, don't you? There's a little place in Chelsea I thought would be rather fun this evening.
Diana (*a young sexual goddess in Henry's eyes*) Oh dear, I'm afraid the glorious Tosser Pilkington-Brick is having an pretty inglorious game.
Paul Have you noticed, Henry, Tosser Pilkington-Brick seems smaller than he did on the playing fields of Dalton?

A whistle blows

Lampo For this relief much thanks.
Diana Not auspicious, folks. Will England recover?

Mrs Hargreaves organizes the picnic during the following

Mr Hargreaves It looks as if young Pilkington-Brick is nervous. What do
  you think, Henry?
Henry To be perfectly honest, Dr Hargreaves, I think my old school hero
  looks like a great, incompetent, unimaginative oaf. Today could go down
  in history as the day Tosser Pilkington-Brick, who I fagged for, lost the
  match for England.
Paul My father is a Fellow of the Royal College of Surgeons. They call
  themselves mister, not doctor.
Henry For heaven's sake, Paul! I've known you for seven years, we were
  best chums at Dalton, your family took me on holiday, and now you tell me.
Diana It is good to see you, Henry.

Diana puts her hand under Henry's rug and causes Henry some surprise

Mr Hargreaves Paul was a Second Lieutenant in the army; I forget your
  rank, Henry.
Henry I wasn't an officer.
Mr Hargreaves Oh, I'm sorry.
Henry I'm glad.
Lampo I was a sergeant in the Education Corps. Priceless. Opportunities for
  mime artists were minimal.

No-one laughs

  Surreal self-mockery, Mr Hargreaves.
Mr Hargreaves So I assumed.
Lampo Ah. Well, I'm at Cambridge now, though it's terribly banal.
Mr Hargreaves Why are you glad you weren't an officer?
Henry Tubman-Edwards, who I happened to be at prep school with, walked
  over to me, up to my elbows in a sink full of filthy grease, freezing cold
  water and vast cooking-tins, and said, "How are you enjoying the army,
  Private Pratt?" I said, "Very much, thank you, sir", knowing that if I'd said
  what I felt like saying I'd have been on a charge. I'd hate to have been an
  officer and been forced to force anyone to say things like that.
Mrs Hargreaves But surely military discipline is very good for one?
Henry Aagh!

Diana smiles

Sorry. National Service will have taught a whole generation to say, "Thank you very much, sir", while meaning, "Sod off you stupid twit", and imbued them with every four-letter word except work.

Diana (*aside to Henry*) You're tense. Relax. This is 1956 after all.

Henry I love you with all my heart, Diana.

Diana (*removing her hand abruptly*) Henry, I find you very appealing, but you could never be that important to me.

Henry Diana, what I probably meant was that I feel all the feelings of love towards you except love itself.

Diana Oh, that's all right, then. (*She puts her hand back under the rug*)

Mrs Hargreaves Do you have decent restaurants in Thurmarsh?

Henry We don't have much of anything in Thurmarsh.

Lampo Ah, traitor.

Diana Except spittle.

Paul Diana!

Henry There is a lot of pneumoconiosis.

Diana I think that's such a beautiful word.

Henry It must be a great consolation to the people who are dying of it.

Lampo Perhaps not such a traitor after all.

Diana Sorry. I thought it was parrots, anyway.

Mr Hargreaves That's psittacosis.

Paul What's psoriasis, then?

Mr Hargreaves A skin disease.

Mrs Hargreaves What has happened to your idea of proper subjects for a picnic at a rugby match!

Lampo Henry, come to Italy with me.

Henry What?

Lampo In the summer. No strings attached. I know how horrified you are by the homosexual side of your nature.

Henry Lampo!

Lampo In Runcorn or Barnsley I might try, to take my mind off the surroundings, but no, Italy's too beautiful for sex.

Henry Have you been to Barnsley?

Lampo I've offended the Yorkshireman in you. I notice you don't defend Runcorn. Let me show you Italy.

Diana Could parrots have psoriasis as well as psittacosis?

Mr Hargreaves Diana!

Henry Aagh!

Mrs Hargreaves Why are you in such a silly mood today?

Diana Because I haven't told Henry that I'm engaged to that great unimaginative oaf Tosser Pilkington-Brick.

Mrs Hargreaves That nickname, really. I thought you knew, Henry?

Lampo Don't be too jealous. He'll either bore her to death or crush her to death.

The Lights cross-fade to:

SCENE 8

Backstage at the Temperance Hall, Haddock Road

Popular music and radio news extracts play as the scene changes

We see bits of the setting for "The Desert Song"; flats, braces, an archway and treads made from beer crates and planks. The finale still hangs in the air

Henry, Cousin Hilda and Ginny Fenwick are waiting

Hilda I thought it were very nice. In parts.
Ginny It was.
Henry Yes.
Ginny Liar.
Henry It was the best performance of *The Desert Song* I've seen at the Temperance Hall, Haddock Road, Thurmarsh, this winter.

Roger enters carrying a pile of chorus dresses. He is the Stage Manager, a florid man. He smiles and crosses the stage

Roger Hallo!

The others ignore him

Roger exits

Hilda It was a pity my friend Mrs Wedderburn couldn't have been here this evening. She has a great talent for sympathy.
Henry Did I introduce you properly? Ginny Fenwick, a friend of mine, Cousin Hilda.
Hilda Henry always were ashamed of his relatives.
Henry I'm not.
Ginny D'you think Barry Frost has to go to Morocco to get changed?
Hilda That make-up must take some getting off. (*She sniffs*)
Ginny (*to Hilda*) Are you coming with us to the pub?
Hilda Certainly not! You're a journalist, I take it?
Ginny Yes, I love it. I want to be a war correspondent. In a few years when I'm ready.
Henry I can just picture you in army boots and a helmet.
Hilda Henry!

Henry I didn't mean just army boots and a helmet.
Hilda Henry!

Roger enters, with a camel. He crosses the stage

Roger For the next one we're at the Civic Hall, you know. Can't wait. Makes the facilities here look amateur.

Roger exits

Hilda Henry doesn't have a fiancée. Does tha, Henry?
Henry (*in disbelief and embarrassment*) Cousin Hilda!
Hilda Tha's started drinking, but I don't know if tha's started — tha knows, courtin'.
Henry Is this what happens when you see an amateur musical?
Hilda Ee, I were being sociable, Henry Pratt. (*She sniffs*) And helpful.
Henry Well, Ginny, how's about a bit of hanky-panky?

Hilda is horrified, Ginny is highly amused and Henry is pleased with himself

Ginny Henry's moving in with me, Hilda.
Hilda What!
Henry No! Ginny!
Ginny What?
Henry That wasn't funny. Cousin Hilda, I'm moving into Ginny's house.
Hilda Aagh!
Henry A flat in her house. Not moving in with her. Ginny was joking.
Ginny Our relationship is strictly platonic.
Henry For the time being. Strictly platonic. I'm moving out next weekend. I've rented a small flat, a very small flat, near here, in the Fish Hill area. And it's in the same house as Ginny, quite coincidentally. Nothing to do with me liking her. Which I do, of course, but it's completely coincidental. I'm sorry, I was going to break it to you gently. I'm not looking forward to it or anything.
Hilda It's your life.

Barry Frost enters, still in costume

Barry No autographs. No autographs.
Henry You aren't changed?
Barry I tend to delay my return to the real world, Henry. Well?

Roger enters carrying a large, empty tea urn, with packets of sugar and tea and a tin of coffee, plus an extension lead and adaptor plug

Roger Some people'd nick anything.
Barry Roger, Roger, how goes it?
Roger It's borrowed and I have to take it home every night. Still, it'll be a
  lock-up counter job at the Civic. It's Mr Frost, Barry, we have to thank. A
  council officer knows the right strings to pull, eh? A nudge and wink's
  worth a pile of correct procedures up at Town Hall. Of course this building
  should have been condemned years ago anyway.

  The others ignore him

  Roger exits

Barry Come on, what did you think?
Hilda The scenery didn't wobble nearly as much as when the Baptist Players
  put on Noël Coward's "Blithe Fever".
Barry Oh, good.
Hilda But I heard every word tha said, Mr Frost.
Barry Thank you.
Hilda I thought you and the prompter were the clearest of all.
Ginny You showed terrific presence of mind, if you don't mind me saying
  so, when the door fell down. You just opened the hole in the wall and
  stepped over the door as if nothing had gone wrong.
Henry Barry Frost, Ginny Fenwick. A friend. Of mine.
Ginny May I talk to you about your aspirations as a planning officer and as
  an artiste?
Barry See you in the pub, Henry.

  Barry and Ginny exit, arm in arm

Hilda I thought she was tha … (*She sniffs*)
Henry He's still got his costume on.

  The Lights cross-fade to:

SCENE 9

Henry's new, small flat in the same house where Ginny lives

*Radio news extracts play as the scene changes and an amateur tenor sings
"My Desert is Waiting" in a Midlands accent*

*From upstairs, the sound of energetic bedsprings accompanies the rhythm
of the singing*

Henry enters with his Auntie Doris, all fur and perfume. Frozen with embarrassment, they try to work out how to deal with the situation. Doris has the first go

Doris Someone enjoys singing.

Henry Ginny's friend. Upstairs. He used to be one of Cousin Hilda's gentlemen.

Doris Cousin Hilda? She'd be surprised.

Henry Ginny's a journalist too. She has a pogo stick.

Doris I said to Geoffrey, you're manning the bar, then I threw on my glad rags and deserted the countryside for the day. I told him Henry must be dying to show his Auntie Doris his new flat. The area around here isn't quite as select as you'd like, I expect.

Henry Fish Hill is my Thurmarsh.

Doris Oh, I know, it's quite near Paradise Lane, where you were born. There is something romantic about slums, I've always said so.

Henry I live opposite the oldest shop in Europe to be in continuous use as a chemist's.

Doris Fascinating. So, this is it. Bijou, isn't it? Bijou.

Henry Not to say cramped and dingy.

Doris So what if it isn't Buckingham Palace? Good heavens, next thing you'll be whipping yourself for not having a personality!

Henry Uncle Teddy used to tell you off for making things worse by protesting about them.

Doris Ah, fancy you remember that. No, this is lovely and I don't mind the musty smell one little bit.

Henry I felt awful moving out of Cousin Hilda's.

Doris How is the sniffer?

Henry Better than she lets on. She hasn't frightened any horses lately.

Doris I've failed you, Henry.

Henry Have you? I'm glad you came on your own.

Doris You don't like Geoffrey very much, do you?

Henry I met Uncle Teddy.

Doris Good Lord. I knew he'd come out, of course.

Henry He's opening a night club. He's calling it the *Cap Ferrat*. After the place where you spent your holidays. Actually, I sort of asked him if he'd ever thought of trying to get you back.

Doris You didn't?

Henry He was encouraging. Very encouraging indeed.

Doris What did he say?

Henry He changed the subject. I mean, he could have said, "That bloody bitch! After what she's done to me?"

Doris Henry!

Henry But he didn't. I do love you, you know.

Doris I don't deserve it, Henry.

Henry I wish you'd waited for Uncle Teddy and I wish you were still with him.

Doris (*contemplating the ceiling*) Bit inconsiderate, that — er, noise, with thin walls.

Henry Depressing too, after the first few hours.

Doris Is it always the same song?

Henry No. He's auditioning for *No, No, Nanette* next week.

Doris I know I've never loved Geoffrey the way I loved Teddy, but Geoffrey couldn't run the hotel without me. He can't keep staff.

Henry The reason he can't keep staff is because he can't keep his hands off them! Lorna told me. He touches her up and makes it look accidental.

There is a slight pause

Doris Arrange for me to see Teddy, will you Henry?

From outside there is a scream of brakes and a thunderous crash as a vehicle smashes into a building

Aagh!

Henry (*looking out of the window*) It's that Old Apothecary's Shop! A lorry has practically demolished it. There's two nuns cowering against the wall. I think they've been hurt.

Doris I've always thought it's unnatural nuns going shopping and standing in bus queues.

Henry comes away from the window and grabs his coat

Henry Auntie Doris, kettle, tea. A reporter is always on call!

Henry rushes out

The Lights cross-fade to:

SCENE 10

The "Cap Ferrat" Nightclub

Popular music and radio news extracts play as the scene changes

The nightclub is in a state of half-preparedness

Henry is talking to Teddy

Henry Will you be my contact from the shady underworld?
Teddy Bloody hell.
Henry I'm not a kid, Teddy. I want to make that clear. I know you were a
black-marketeer in the war.
Teddy Don't mention Rangoon again.
Henry I won't. (*A slight pause*) I've been looking for you everywhere, since
I met you in the café.
Teddy I've been in France, picking up last-minute items. All genuine stuff.
I hope I can rely on you for a good spread in paper.
Henry Only the best.
Teddy Well, what's this all about?
Henry I wanted to drop it casually into the conversation.
Teddy What?
Henry Oh, nothing. Come to think of it I don't suppose there's much point
in you and me discussing anything. For one thing I imagine you're pretty
right-wing and everything. Villains usually are. Uncle Teddy, I do, er —
love you, you know. I just want make that clear.
Teddy I don't deserve it. Don't stand there with the weight of the world's
shortcomings on your shoulders. It'll destroy you. You're right about
villains though; I wonder why?
Henry All left-wingers are left-wingers either because they are poor, or
because they are idealists. Not many villains are idealists, and not many of
them are poor.
Teddy You can be quite clever sometimes.
Henry I know, so why is my life such a mess?
Teddy I've failed you.
Henry Why do people keep saying that to me?
Teddy If I hadn't had to take that trip to Rangoon you could have stayed at
Dalton public school and the world would have been your oyster on a plate
at your feet.
Henry I've only just realized that my travels round the class system were
criminally financed. I don't dislike you, Teddy.
Teddy That's big of you.
Henry No, I just wanted to make that clear as well. Actually I think maybe
I'm fatally fascinated by evil.
Teddy Henry, you were a berk as a child and you still are.
Henry Ah. (*A slight pause*) You know your colleague, the one I met in the
café that Saturday morning …
Teddy Derek Parsonage? What about him?
Henry He reminded me of Auntie Doris's "fancy man", as Cousin Hilda
calls him, that's all.

Teddy Derek reminded you of Geoffrey Porringer?
Henry Blackheads. Both their noses are festooned with blackheads. I'm
sorry, I shouldn't be rude about your friends.
Teddy Henry! Derek I do count as a friend but Geoffrey Porringer? Hardly.
I'm the idiot who thought he was a trusted accomplice while all the time
he was spending intimate afternoons in bed with my wife as was!
Henry Sorry. I've talked to Auntie Doris.
Teddy It'd have been rude not to. (*A slight pause*) Are you going to spit it
out or what, Henry?
Henry Do you think it possible you could ever have her back?

The Lights cross-fade to:

SCENE 11

Cousin Hilda's basement living-room

Popular music and radio news extracts play as the scene changes

Cousin Hilda, holding a scrapbook, addresses Mr O'Reilly

Hilda Mr O'Reilly, have I shown you our Henry's scrapbook?
Mr O'Reilly Oh yes, I t'ink you did.
Hilda No, I haven't, Mr O'Reilly, I haven't at all.
Mr O'Reilly No, that's right, you didn't.
Hilda I'm expecting tha to respect my confidence, Mr O'Reilly.
Mr O'Reilly Oh yes.
Hilda He'd be right embarrassed if he knew. It's for him, to look back when
he's older.
Mr O'Reilly Oh yes.
Hilda I don't want tha to think I'm boasting. And tha knows I don't hold
wi' sentimental nonsense. Did I tell tha he visits me regular?
Mr O'Reilly I t'ink you did.
Hilda No I didn't, Mr O'Reilly, I didn't at all.
Mr O'Reilly That's right, you didn't.
Hilda Well he does. Often.
Mr O'Reilly Oh yes.
Hilda When tha's not in.
Mr O'Reilly I was wondering why I hadn't seen him.
Hilda Does tha want to look at scrapbook or not, Mr O'Reilly?
Mr O'Reilly Oh yes.

They look at the book

Hilda Look, (*she reads*) "Chiropodist Breaks Foot." "Man, Eighty-Three, Falls Out of Bed."
Mr O'Reilly (*reading*) "British Military Police Kill Cypriot Youth."
Hilda What? No, Henry's is on't back, Mr O'Reilly.
Mr O'Reilly (*reading*) "Cuff Links Found After Forty-Two Years."
Hilda Is tha listening, Mr O'Reilly? (*She reads*) "A seventy-six year old diabetic retired railway guard was making an amazing recovery today in Thurmarsh Infirmary after lying semi-conscious in a rhubarb patch for ten hours only yards from the council pre-fab in which his wife Gladys and their Jack Russell, Spot, were waiting anxiously for his return from a Darby and Joan hot-pot supper and whist drive."
Mr O'Reilly Oh yes.
Hilda (*reading*) "Treasured Old Apothecary's Shop Damaged Beyond Repair. Demolition imminent. Local lorry driver, Arnold Nutley, twenty-nine, known to his friends as Tree-Trunk Nutley ..." "Tree-Trunk Nutley"?
Mr O'Reilly What's "thives"?
Hilda A misprint. Mr O'Reilly! (*She reads*) "... Tree-Trunk Nutley had a miraculous escape when he crashed into Thurmarsh's oldest historical landmark narrowly missing two buns."

Hilda and Mr O'Reilly puzzle

The Lights cross-fade to:

SCENE 12

The "Cap Ferrat" nightclub

Popular music and radio news extracts play as the scene changes

The club has traditional fake southern French décor

Henry and Neil sit at different tables

Uncle Teddy makes an announcement, off

Teddy (*off*) Let's make this an opening night to remember! Some good old Yorkshire meaty grit with a dash of French sauce! There's great big dollops of that here at the Cap Ferrat. And now, more from Alphonso Boycott and his Northern Serenaders!

A band plays a slightly naughty dance tune slightly naughtily

Colin enters

Colin Why do I have this fatal impulse towards self-destruction?
Henry What are you talking about, Colin?
Colin I'm about to put my life in danger.
Henry Thurmarsh isn't Chicago, Colin.
Colin It isn't Tunbridge Wells either.
Henry You daft twit.

Colin exits

Helen enters

I hear we're going to have the legendary Martine later. She's a cross
between Marlene Dietrich and Edith Piaf.
Helen It's a cross we are going to have to bear. I want to mark your card.
Henry Pardon?
Helen For a dance. Sex makes us all selfish.
Neil (*to Helen*) I want to mark your card.
Helen Shut up, Neil.

Helen exits

Ginny enters

Ginny I hear we are going to have the *Côte D'Azur Cuties* from the French
coast.
Henry Well, near the French coast. Folkestone.
Ginny I've been meaning to mention this. Do you ever hear me — er —
us … ?
Henry Throwing yourselves round your bed in orgies of sexual excitement
to the accompaniment of selections from the musicals? Yes, a lot.
Ginny Oh Lord. I hope it hasn't ——
Henry Kept me awake, wallowing in loneliness and frustration, night after
agonizing night?
Ginny Oh Lord. Henry, I never had anything like this. I can't give it up.
Henry It's all right; sex makes us all selfish.

Ginny exits

Neil moves over to Henry

Neil I think you like Ginny, and I think she likes you. I don't think you should
give up hope. Forget Helen, though.
Henry I was going to say the same thing to you, Neil.

Neil exits

Teddy enters with a copy of the "Argus"

Teddy I've a damn good mind to throttle you. (*He reads*) "Among the celebrities invited to join the first night festivities are Kenneth Horne, Maurice Chevalier ——"
Henry Have they come?
Teddy No, you pillock! I only wrote to them for the publicity. (*He reads*) " ... also Danielle Darrieux, Michael Venison and Dulcie Crab. It should be quite a fight."
Henry "Night." "Michael Denison and Dulcie Gray."
Teddy I know who they are!
Henry Misprints, I'm afraid.
Teddy You've done this deliberately. If one more customer asks me how the fight is going with Michael Venison and Dulcie Crab, you won't get out of here alive, young man!

Teddy exits

Ben enters

Henry (*staring off*) Oh Lord, I don't believe it! Just come in. That's Sergeant Botney! From my national service!
Ben Are you all right? You look as if you've seen a ghost.
Henry Ben, what did you do in the war?
Ben I was a conscientious objector. I worked down the mines.
Henry I'm sorry.
Ben What d'you mean?
Henry I'm sorry for everything I ever thought.
Ben Stop being so big-headed. 'Ere, how many first division footballers have Edwin as either a first or second name?
Henry None.
Ben Correct.
Henry Talking to you has made up my mind, Ben.

Ben exits

Colin enters

Colin I have danced with someone!
Henry I saw, she was quite something.
Colin I've danced with Bill Holliday's girlfriend.

Henry You mean the scrap king of the Rundle Valley?

Colin Leader of the Thurmarsh Mafia.

Henry Rich.

Colin Powerful.

Henry Evil.

Colin I've danced with the voluptuous Angela Groyne. I'm a dead man, Henry.

Colin exits

Teddy (*announcing, off*) And now, the *Cap Ferrat*'s resident dancing girls, the *Côte D'Azur Cuties*!

The four "Côte D'Azur Cuties" enter and perform

Sergeant Botney enters

Botney (*calling off*) Hey! How's the fight going with Michael Venison and Dulcie Crab?

Henry I was in your hut, Sergeant.

Botney Ah. How do, lad.

Henry (*apparently joking*) I've never forgotten that first night, Sarge. We made bed-packs. You said they were terrible. You threw them out of the window. It was raining. They landed on wet flower beds. We fetched them. You said, "Lights out." We made our wet, dirty beds in the dark at one o'clock in the morning.

Botney My job was to make a man of you. I did a good job.

Henry The things you did. You still make me nervous. But I was the one who found him, you see. You don't even remember, do you? The late Signal-man Burbage. He hanged himself in our hut. Because of you. You didn't make a man out of Burbage, did you?

Botney This is my wedding anniversary, lad, the wife'll be through in a minute!

Henry We all agreed, whichever one of us met you in civvie street. It's me, Sergeant. You're not stupid, and that's why it's all so inexcusable, you sadistic, murdering bastard!

Henry throws his drink in Sergeant Botney's face. The "Côte D'Azur Cuties" falter

The Lights cross-fade to:

Outside the Cap Ferrat

Popular music and radio news extracts play as the scene changes

We hear fire engines, crowds, ladders, fire-hoses; see flames roaring into the night sky

Henry and Ginny enter, Henry with his outdoor clothes over his pyjamas

Ginny Quick, Henry! It's here! It's round here, Rock-Salmon Avenue.

Henry (*exhausted from running*) It's all right for you, you're a fashion correspondent in training to be a war correspondent.

Ginny You wanted a scoop, didn't you? Oh my God!

Henry *The Cap Ferrat*! Uncle Teddy's new nightclub.

Ginny I had a feeling.

Henry So did I.

George Timpley, a pale tobacconist, enters

Henry moves to leave and is restrained by Ginny

Ginny You can't go in there, Henry!

Henry It's my uncle's club!

Ginny The firemen are doing their best. Keep out of their road, for Christ's sake!

Timpley Oh my God.

Henry I know, and it only opened two weeks ago.

Timpley I'm not insured.

Henry Have you seen my uncle, have you seen Teddy Braithwaite?

Timpley I forgot to renew the insurance.

Ginny What?

Henry Has anyone seen my uncle, Teddy Braithwaite?

Timpley The insurance on Timpley's, the tobacconist's. Timpley and Nephews. Between the nightclub and the Thurmarsh Joke Emporium and Magic Shop. That's my livelihood there. That's thirty-three years. They say the whole block may go.

Henry (*scribbling in his notebook*) "Tobacconist watched as his life's work went up to smoke."

Helen Cornish enters. She is immaculate

Helen Have you phoned the nationals? You get paid "lineage", you know.
Henry (*to George Timpley*) Do you know Mr Braithwaite, the owner? Have you heard anything? Is he in there?
Helen Oh my God. I'm here to support you, Henry.

Derek Parsonage enters from the fire

Derek The magic shop's in grave danger.
Henry Derek Parsonage! Do you know anything?
Helen I've been in that shop. The street will be full of fake cakes, bottomless tumblers, diminishing Woodbines and impossible spoons.
Derek It'll be the tobacconist's next.
Timpley Oh my God.
Ginny (*to the heavens*) If you exist, which I doubt, let Timpley and Nephews survive this night.
Timpley That shop is my dream.
Henry (*writing again*) "Tobacconist's pipe dream goes up in smoke." How can I find out if Teddy's all right?
Derek They don't reckon anyone was left in there. It was all locked up.
Henry Thank heavens. Mr Timpley, may I ask your first name?
Timpley George. Oh my God. Why?
Henry How old are you, George?
Timpley Fifty-seven. Oh my God. Why?

There is small explosion off and a box with a label lands at Derek's feet. He picks it up

Derek (*reading*) "Naughty Fido Dog Turds, to be collected; the Winstanley Young Conservatives."
Helen Henry, it's a good story, but it'll be an even better one if his shop burns down.
Ginny I'm going to phone the *Daily Herald*.
Helen We'll do the others.
Ginny How many appliances, d'you think?

Ginny exits

Helen Seventeen, twenty-two, twenty, eighteen. Really! Make it look as if it comes from different sources.

Colin enters dramatically, with black eyes and bandages

Colin! Whatever's happened?

Colin He who dances with Angela Groyne pays the piper. Bill Holliday's revenge.

There are ominous creaks, off

Derek Oh my God! There goes the joke shop!

There is an explosion. The contents of the joke shop fall through the air and land on stage: trick cigars, funny noses, sneezing powder, plastic fried eggs. Helen falls over on to a farting cushion; this does nothing for her dignity. Henry finds this very funny

Helen Don't laugh! Henry, Colin, this is sneezing powder. I'm distraught, Henry, for God's sake!

Auntie Doris enters. Her face and limbs are blackened and her clothing is in shreds

Henry Auntie Doris!
Doris I'm distraught, Henry, for God's sake!
Henry Auntie Doris, what are you doing here?
Doris I came to meet him! I came to meet him! Henry, he's in there!
Derek No, no, it was all locked up.
Doris Yes, but I was to knock three times! It was all arranged.
Henry
Helen
George } (*together*) Oh my God!
Colin
Derek
Doris Teddy is burning alive in the *Cap Ferrat*!

They stare off in the light from the fire

Popular music and radio news extracts play

Fade to Black-out

ACT II

SCENE 1

The porch of the Church of the Holy Trinity, Rowth Bridge

Popular music and radio news extracts play. This fades to be replaced by the sound of an organ playing enthusiastically within the church — but with little regard for accuracy

The Lights come up

The slimy Geoffrey Porringer waits, anxiously looking at his watch, with the Rev. Peter Hazard, the vicar

Geoffrey We wanted it small.
The Rev. And small it is, Mr — Er ...
Geoffrey Geoffrey. Please. Geoffrey Porringer. You only get married once.
The Rev. Really, Mr Porringer.
Geoffrey Well, no, it's my second and Doris's second. Her first husband was burnt to death recently. (*A slight pause*) It's funny, isn't it, but we could have invited lots of customers — but, once you've started, where do you stop?
The Rev. Another wedding is due in soon.
Geoffrey Doris'll be here before you could embroider your cassock.

Henry and Cousin Hilda enter from the church, both done up for the wedding

Oh, Reverend Hazard, I don't know if you've met Doris's nephew, Henry, who she treated as a son before her husband had to go to Rangoon and her cousin, Hilda, who's his mother now?
Hilda How d'you do, I'm sure. Trust our Doris. (*She sniffs*)
Henry Minor hiccup on an otherwise glorious occasion, Mr Porringer.
Geoffrey Oh "Geoffrey", please. We're making it legal now, young sir.

Hilda sniffs

If she ever gets here.

Henry (*to Geoffrey*) You know, Geoffrey … Uncle Geoffrey ——
Geoffrey (*touched*) Well, young sir!
Henry You should be extra specially grateful I've honoured you with my
    presence because two of my best friends are also getting married today, at
    Thurmarsh Registry Office: Ted Plunkett and Helen Cornish.
Geoffrey I hope they will be very happy.
Henry (*to himself*) Oh, Helen.
The Rev. Let me know if she deigns to arrive.

The Rev. leaves

Geoffrey (*following the Rev.*) She'll be here before you could starch your
    dog collar.

Geoffrey exits

Hilda I should have thrown the invitation to her wedding with that slimy
    person, while her husband is practically still warm, in the dustbin!
Henry Something puzzles me, Cousin Hilda. I'm not a Christian any more,
    but I can forgive. You are and you can't.
Hilda I'm here, aren't I? Self-righteousness is a sin an'all, Henry Pratt.
Henry Hilda, I've got to bow out of Filey.
Hilda Bow out of Filey!
Henry I thought I could go with you but I've been invited to go on holiday
    with a chap I used to fag for at Dalton.
Hilda Him what plays wi'oval balls?
Henry Not Tosser Pilkington-Brick, it's Lampo Davey who shared a study
    with him and who I also fagged for. He practically begged me to join him
    on holiday abroad. It's just after I come back from my compulsory
    Territorial Army training which doesn't count towards my holiday be-
    cause it's compulsory.
Hilda I don't hold wi'abroad.
Henry Lampo Davey is a guest at another wedding today as well. In
    Kensington. Diana Hargreaves is marrying Tosser Pilkington-Brick. I was
    invited but I couldn't, naturally.
Hilda I hope they'll both be very happy, I'm sure.
Henry (*to himself*) Oh, Diana!

Geoffrey enters

Geoffrey It's funny, isn't it, how men of the cloth panic at the slightest
    opportunity. Well, young sir, you're looking well.

Hilda sniffs

And you are. Rowth Bridge must be full of memories for you, young sir.

Henry I met my first girlfriend in Rowth Bridge. I was eight and an evacuee. She was called Lorna Arrow and lived here.
Geoffrey Funny, isn't it?
Henry She was your last waitress.
Geoffrey Oh, that Lorna Arrow. I remember her.

Doris enters. She wears a large hat and is radiant in the extreme

Doris Hilda, Henry, Geoffrey!
Geoffrey (*to Hilda and Henry*) Look as if you weren't worried.
Doris Whatever are you doing outside? You've spoiled it now.
Geoffrey Doris!
Doris Don't clench your teeth at me, Geoffrey. I was going to signal privately to the organist.

Hilda sniffs

What's that supposed to mean?
Hilda What's what supposed to mean?
Doris At moments of disapproval you sniff, Hilda. To what particular disapproval do we owe that particular snorter?

Hilda struggles to retain her composure — and loses

Hilda Ee, don't start me off! Henry, tha should never have persuaded me to come.
Henry Cousin Hilda!
Hilda Shameless isn't the word. Marrying a man tha ran off with while tha husband's charred body's still smouldering in his grave! (*She regains her self-control*) It's a day of joy and I'll not cast a cloud. I've been unChristian enough already. I hope you'll both be very happy.
Doris We'll chat at the reception, Hilda. Small but refined. So it's just you and those frustrated men in your house now your little bird's flown the coop. Must be much more convenient now he's not under your feet.

Hilda sniffs with inexpressible rage

Doris and Geoffrey, Henry and Hilda exit

Wedding music plays, off, full of wonder and inaccuracies

Eric Lugg enters, dressed as a bridegroom. He looks uncomfortable and has a pint in his hand

There is a pause

Fred Hathersage enters, with a cigar. He looks at gravestones during the following

Fred Haven't clapped eyes on Rebecca Hathersage, has tha?
Eric What does she look like?
Fred Terrible. She died in 1932. I mean her tombstone.
Eric I don't know owt about it. I'm waiting for me wedding.
Fred Is tha? Is tha really?
Eric Aye.
Fred There's one born every minute.
Eric 'Ere … !
Fred (*looking again*) Me old mother is convinced Rebecca were buried in this churchyard. Wants to be laid to rest along of her when the time comes. Me mam lives in't village. I visit her regular as clockwork, every alternate August.

Doris, Geoffrey and Henry enter

Henry throws an embarrassed handful of confetti over Doris and Geoffrey. During the following, Henry takes photographs of the couple

Hey up, they're out, it's tha turn for t'dentist.
Doris Wasn't it beautiful, Henry?
Fred (*to Eric*) Nice setting for it. I enjoy a good ruin.
Doris (*overhearing*) Geoffrey!
Geoffrey I don't think he was referring to the bride, Doris. Where's Hilda?
Henry Admiring the brasses.
Fred (*to Eric*) A bit of decay gives atmosphere to a place. But only in t'country. In t'towns I like it gleaming. Cities of the future. Cities of glass. Fred Hathersage is the name, I'm in property.

Henry cannot concentrate on taking photographs as he is distracted by Fred Hathersage

Geoffrey Photos, young sir.
Henry (*producing his notebook; to Fred*) Mr Hathersage, Pratt of the *Argus*, we haven't met. You're on the board of Thurmarsh United?
Fred Aye, and bloody proud of it. Whatever tha wants to know tha's come to t'right man.
Henry What d'you think of the rumoured departure of Tommy Marsden?
Fred No comment.

Henry What d'you think about Fish Hill, a run down area of great local character much loved by the people of Thurmarsh and coincidentally where I live? Is it due for redevelopment?

Fred No comment.

Doris Wasn't it beautiful, Geoffrey? Teddy would have appreciated it so much.

Geoffrey Doris! Could we refrain from considering the likely opinions of your accidentally cremated dead husband for this day in particular?

Doris Oh, touchy!

Eric (*to Fred*) You're the bloke wi't'Rolls Royce what comes t'Rowth Bridge Bottom every alternate August? Flash bastard.

Fred (*to Eric*) I develop property, lad. Buildings have to have a front, so do folks. If people such as you want work, it has to be fresh salmon and lobster thermidor for me, when I long for fish and chips, actually.

Fred exits

Doris (*aside to Henry*) I know what you're thinking, Henry. Fate thwarted us with a faulty fire-extinguisher.

Lorna Arrow enters, dressed as a bride

All (*except Lorna*) Lorna Arrow!

Lorna Hallo, Mr Porringer.

Doris Oh, one of our ex-waitresses.

Lorna Hallo, Mrs Braithwaite.

Doris Née Braithwaite, née née Elgin, my maiden name but no connection with the marbles. It's Mrs Porringer now, Lorna.

Geoffrey Lorna used to be a great friend of Henry's.

Doris We'd best draw a veil over that.

Eric Weren't that the job you left very suddenly?

Doris We'd best draw a veil over that too.

Lorna Hallo, Eric.

Henry Eric Lugg!

Lorna D'you remember, Henry?

Eric Oh aye, I do now. I used to call him "evacuee squirt".

Henry Lorna and me were good friends once; before your time, of course.

Doris Henry, fancy Lorna marrying Eric Lugg.

Eric What does tha mean, "before my time?"

Doris Geoffrey.

Geoffrey We'll go on.

Doris Henry, don't dawdle. The cold buffet'll get warm.

Doris and Geoffrey exit

Eric (*with more than a hint of menace*) There never was a time before my
    time.
Henry No, no. Oh no. Of course there wasn't. I just meant, I liked Lorna. She
    liked ——
Lorna Oh, Henry!
Eric 'Ere, what's going on?
Lorna Eric, put a sock in it.
Eric (*putting his arm round Henry*) Right, then. Come wi'us in t'church.
Henry I'm waiting for my aunt, er I mean, cousin. The warm buffet'll get
    cold.
Eric No, no. Me mate's passed out under t'bridge, I need a best man.
Henry Oh, Lorna!

The Lights cross-fade to:

SCENE 2

The interior of a large tent, somewhere in Yorkshire

*Popular music and radio news extracts play as the scene changes. Rain beats
on the canvas*

*Henry is in bed. He is having a nightmare. Signalman Brian Furnace — a
vision — is hidden under the sheets. There is another body — a dummy — in
another bed, motionless*

Henry sits up in bed

Sergeant Botney enters

Henry You can't do National Service twice, Sarge.
Botney You can if the authorities say so, laddie. And they say so! They've
    decided they need you. Gawd knows why.
Henry But I have a great career ahead of me as a reporter, Sergeant.
Botney Well now you have a great career ahead of you as a soldier, sunshine.
    Who are you?

Brian appears from under Henry's sheets

Brian Signalman Brian Furnace, Sarge.
Botney Two soldiers in one pit! Two naked signalmen in one pit! I've never
    seen anything like it. What's going on?
Brian We love each other.

Botney You what? You love each other? This is the British Army. You're on a charge. Filthy, idle and stark-bollock-naked on parade. Get down to the parade room. You dirty little buggers!

The body of a young man — the dummy — shoots up from inside the other bed and hangs swinging high above their heads

Henry screams

Get down from there, Signalman Burbage! Committing suicide on duty. I'll have you for this! This is the British Army, you wanker! (*He shouts an order*) Squad will laugh at Signalman Burbage. Squad — wait for it — squad — at Signalman Burbage — laugh!

Henry and Brian obey the order. Hundreds of other unseen squaddies join in

The body vanishes, Botney and Brian vanish

The rain stops, dawn breaks and the birds sing

Henry gets up and gets dressed during the following

Officer (*through a megaphone; off*) Erm, good-morning, men. Erm, we were going to have a demonstration of — erm, flame throwers, which I think you would have all found very — erm, interesting … but apparently — well, we're rather in the hands of the flame thrower chappies so we'll have to scrub round that one …

Brian enters

However, never fear, we are hoping to arrange — erm, a display of camouflage techniques — which should be jolly interesting. Erm — for the moment, stand easy.

Henry sits down. The two men light cigarettes

Brian They can't make us do another two years, can they?
Henry Course they can't.
Brian Only with the crisis in the Middle East and everything …
Henry Brian, we're here for a fortnight.
Brian Only it's my dad's shop. He's going into hospital with his piles. His bleeding backside's bleeding. I've got to run the shop.

Henry If there's ever general mobilization, you'll probably get exemption on compassionate grounds.

Officer (*through a megaphone; off*) Erm — right, men. Erm — efforts to locate the camouflage team at short notice have unfortunately failed. Perhaps they were too jolly well camouflaged, what? Training in — erm — something else will commence shortly. I believe. So — erm, for the moment, erm — stand easy.

Pause

Brian I'm sorry I didn't write.

Henry Yes, Brian, so am I.

Brian I'm engaged.

Henry What?

Brian To this nurse, from Truro.

Henry Ah. Great.

Brian About, er — us? It was just, you know, the sergeant warning us about loose women and unfortunate consequences and everything.

Henry Yes.

Brian Sorry, Henry.

Henry What?

Brian You're upset, aren't you?

Henry No, Brian, it's just that I was going to say the same thing to you.

Brian What?

Henry About us. And the sergeant and — er …

Brian Oh, well, that's all right, then, isn't it?

Brian exits

Night falls. The rain starts

Henry sleeps

Sergeant Botney, a vision, enters

Botney You're going to be sorry you ruined my wedding anniversary. You've signed on while pissed, sunshine. I'm going to ruin your next fifteen years!

The Lights cross-fade to:

Scene 3

A beautiful street café in the beautiful Piazza del Campo in Siena

Popular music and radio news extracts play as the scene changes

Henry Pratt, podgy, and Lampo Davey, aesthetic, are on holiday

Henry I'm a blank page, Lampo. I have no personality. You wanted me to come to Italy so you could create me in your own image.

Lampo Mawkish rubbish. I wanted you to come to Italy because you are not blasé. With you I can live each day as if it's my last.

Anna Matheson, nubile, and Hilary Lewthwaite, neurotic, enter

Hilary I'm too hot to worry.

Anna I want you to enjoy yourself.

Henry Ah! You're English!

Hilary If we'd wanted to meet English people we'd have gone to Scarborough.

Anna Don't mind her, she's crabby today.

Henry Henry Pratt, Lampo Davey.

Anna Anna Matheson, Hilary Lewthwaite.

Henry The only Lewthwaite I know is a clapped-out draper's in Thurmarsh.

Hilary That's our shop.

Henry When I say clapped-out, I mean I really like it. I love old-fashioned shops. When I was a kid, Lampo, I used to be absolutely fascinated by the thing they had that whizzed the change around on wires.

Hilary The Lamson Overhead Cash System.

Lampo Absolutely fascinating.

Henry You're from Thurmarsh? I can't get over this.

Lampo Do try.

Henry Where are you from, Anna?

Anna Ullapool Grove.

Henry Thurmarsh as well! Isn't this amazing, Lampo?

Lampo Only slightly.

Henry Why don't we share a table?

Anna Great idea.

A waiter enters

Lampo reluctantly explains to the waiter in impeccable Italian that the four of them would like to share a table

Waiter Ah! You share table. Is good.
Henry Where do you live, Hilary?
Hilary Perkin Warbeck Drive.
Lampo Has anyone got a street map of Thurmarsh? No? What a shame. It would have eased the monotony of looking at Siena.
Henry This is a bit different from the Rundle Café. That's a café in Thurmarsh.
Lampo No! It has such a Parisian ring.
Henry You're very quiet, Hilary.

There is a slight pause

Where did you go to school, Anna?
Anna Thurmarsh Grammar.
Henry I don't believe this!
Lampo Oh, I do.
Henry Did you know Karen Porter or Maureen Abberley?
Lampo Oh, good, let's not discuss the beauties of Tuscany and the treasures of the art gallery. Come on, let's talk some more about Karen Porter and Maureen Abberley.
Hilary They're very beautiful.
Anna Karen Porter and Maureen Abberley?
Hilary The paintings.
Henry What about Mr E. F. Crowther!
Hilary Gossip is the last refuge of the small-minded.
Lampo Ah, you're merciless. How attractive.
Henry He vanished.
Anna I know.
Lampo Oh this is far more interesting than the wonderful works of the great Sienese painter Simone Martini.
Henry But what you don't know is that I was the last person to see him alive.
Anna Simone Martini?
Henry Mr E. F. Crowther, my old headmaster. I interviewed him an hour and three-quarters before he vanished. Inexplicably, Lampo.
Anna Forever.
Hilary Last week.
Henry You see, I'm writing a series of pen-portraits on leading local citizens. "Proud Sons of Thurmarsh", actually. I'm a journalist.
Lampo I'm an aesthete.
Hilary I'm on holiday.
Anna I'm interested.
Henry What are you doing this afternoon, Anna? I mean Hilary as well.
Hilary The cathedral.

Anna The cathedral.
Hilary Well, we decided that.
Henry What would you rather do, Anna?
Anna Do you have any suggestions?
Lampo The art gallery.
Henry The art gallery.
Lampo Well, we decided that.
Anna I wouldn't mind going to the art gallery again.
Hilary You said you found the paintings depressing.
Henry We could go to the cathedral again.
Lampo I'm not going to the cathedral again.
Henry You said it was one of the loveliest buildings in Europe.
Lampo It is. I saw it this morning. Big thing with pillars.
Henry You go and see the pictures then. I'll go to the cathedral again.
Lampo I want to see the pictures with you. I'll go back to the room and read; tomorrow we'll look at the pictures.
Hilary Whatever's happening, our bus leaves at five.
Henry You aren't staying in Siena? Look, why don't the girls go to the cathedral, and we'll go to the art gallery, and I'll arrange to meet Anna — and Hilary, later in Thurmarsh?

Henry puts his hand on Anna's knee

Hilary That's that sorted out. Time to go.
Anna Well, this is *arrivederci*.

Various kisses are exchanged all round — almost

Anna and Hilary exit

Lampo Look at you. You're an itching, sweating, frustration-soaked, mosquito-ravaged, immature, repressed English podge-clot diverted from high art by mere fleshy legs.
Henry I know.

Denzil enters

Oh my God!
Denzil I thought you'd chosen Filey.
Henry Lampo Davey, Denzil Ackerman of the Thurmarsh *Evening Argus*.

Lampo and Denzil shake hands; their handshake lasts longer than politeness demands. Henry stares, unable to believe what he is seeing

The Lights cross-fade to:

SCENE 4

The Snug Bar of the "Navigation Inn", Thurmarsh

Popular music and radio news extracts play as the scene changes

Henry is writing in his notebook. Mrs C. E. Jenkinson, landlady, too friendly, is in attendance

Mrs Atkinson Nights are beginning to draw in, I said.
Henry Oh, sorry.
Mrs Jenkinson Tha's not one of my husband's regulars?
Henry Me dad used to be. The *Navigation* were his favourite pub before the war.
Mrs Jenkinson Oh aye.
Henry Me dad and your husband had a bit of a quarrel, Mrs Jenkinson.
Mrs Jenkinson Ezra Pratt. He were tha father.
Henry Yes.
Mrs Jenkinson (*laughing*) Ezra Pratt strangled a parrot the day tha were born. Whole street knew. It were imitating tha mother's labour pains. Laugh? If my husband sees thee he'll boot thee out in t'street.
Henry He gave my dad's place in the dominoes team permanently to another man while he were away fighting Germans.

Anna Matheson enters

Anna Forgive me, I'm late. This is quaint.
Henry It has memories.
Anna I'll have a Pernod.
Henry (*to Mrs Jenkinson*) Er …
Mrs Jenkinson Don't stock it.
Anna Gin and it.
Mrs Jenkinson Coming up.
Anna D'you want to play darts?
Henry Darts? That's not very romantic.
Anna We can be romantic later on.
Henry (*to Mrs Jenkinson*) Could I have some darts?

Mrs Jenkinson gives them some darts; they play darts during the following

Henry This is a bit different from Siena. Oh, what an obvious remark.

Anna Italy was a big mistake. Well, not Italy, Italy's all right. Going with Hilary. I just have this thing about illness.

Henry Is Hilary ill?

Anna In her mind. Poor old Hillers. She finds life so incredibly difficult. Do you find life difficult, Henry?

Henry Incredibly.

Anna Oh God! What is wrong with people? I mean if you're really poor or something like that, fair enough, you should be miserable. But not people like us. What have you to worry about, Henry?

Henry Well, I'm a socialist. Anna, I haven't been able to stop thinking about you.

Anna That's nice. I'm not forward or anything but I can't bear people being tense. When we go back to your flat later I'll take all my clothes off and you can tell me why you're a socialist.

Henry Bloody hell, Anna!

Ben Watkinson and Tommy Marsden enter

Tommy Ben, I ask you, can Muir and Ayers give me the through passes I need if I'm to utilize my speed?

Ben That's a tough one, Tommy.

Tommy Can they buggery. I've got the scoring instincts of a predatory panther, and I'm being sacrificed on the altar of mid-table mediocrity.

Henry Tommy Marsden, tha's bin reading too many press reports.

Tommy By the heck, Henry Pratt!

Ben Oh, Henry!

Anna A friend of yours?

Mrs Jenkinson Tha's only talking to t'star of United. Usual, Tommy?

Tommy Paradise Lane gang, eh?

Mrs Jenkinson All friends of Tommy's are welcome in t' *Navigation*.

Henry Even the son of a parrot strangler?

Ben I owe you an apology, Henry. Tommy's your contact and I've poached him using your name.

Anna Anyone for darts?

Mrs Jenkinson (*handing over more arrows*) They're Cecil's second best. But he won't be too angry.

Tommy I were telling Ben I've got a lethal left foot. So it all adds up. That's why I'm on transfer list.

Ben It's a scoop. I'm sorry, Henry.

Henry You've been on that list a few months, Tommy.

Ben You knew?

Henry Tommy told me before I started on the *Argus*.

Ben That's gone right to my bladder, Henry.

Ben exits

Anna You're leaving Thurmarsh and I've only just met you.

Henry What about loyalty to the town that took an urchin off the streets and turned him into a star?

Tommy Don't make me laugh. One of our directors is busy buying up half t'town centre dirt cheap so he can redevelop it at vast profits. Why shouldn't I look out for myself? I'll just get 'em stacked up.

Henry (*getting his notebook out*) Who, and when and what?

Tommy Chuff me no, I've said enough.

Henry Hang on, it's Fred Hathersage, isn't it? Tommy!

Tommy exits

Anna Where's he gone?

Mrs Jenkinson Through to t'public. Don't worry, he'll be back wi' drinks.

Henry Anna — there's something I want to say to you.

Anna You don't want me to take all my clothes off.

Henry How did you know?

Anna Oh, it happens to me quite a lot.

Henry You're lying.

Anna Yes, it's never happened before in the whole of my life. (*She laughs*) I think you went for the wrong one that day in Siena. Old Hillers is pretty desperate for a man.

Henry Thank you.

Anna She's very serious and high-minded but I think you are too. You're both fairly screwed up.

Henry Thank you.

Anna I think your repressions might be made for each other. I hope you don't mind me saying this?

Henry Oh no. You've made my evening.

Ben enters

Ben I feel terrible about this — he's your life-long friend and so on — but you have to admit, if it was left to you, the only news in the paper would be lost dogs and what's on at the pictures.

Henry That's not how I see myself.

Ben Well, I hope you don't mind me commenting?

Henry Just you wait and see, Ben. I might be on the trail of a scoop that'll blow the lid off this town.

Tommy enters with a tray full of drinks

Ben Name all the teams in the Wartime League North.

Mrs Jenkinson 'Ere, my Cecil could do that!

Anna Couldn't you have got the drinks in here, Tommy?

Tommy Me fans are in there. I wait till I'm congratulated on my last amazing goal and they say, "What you 'aving then, Tommy?" And I say, "A glass of usual and some for me friends." Never fails.

Anna Who's beating me at darts, then?

Henry I'll just concentrate on supping.

Anna, Ben and Tommy play darts. Henry is feeling very sorry for himself. During the following, Anna and Tommy talk confidentially, leaving Ben isolated

Mrs Jenkinson Tha mother were Ada, weren't she? Knocked down by a bus on t'way to meet thy father on leave.

Henry Aye, Mrs Jenkinson.

Mrs Jenkinson Ada's stuck-up sister, Doris, married Teddy Braithwaite. Him what went to prison for fraud.

Henry Black market, Mrs Jenkinson. It were the war.

Mrs Jenkinson My Cecil still can't stand mention of your father. He'd have you an' all if he walked through that door. Went a bit funny in t'head, didn't he? Your father? Ezra Pratt?

Henry What, Mrs Jenkinson?

Mrs Jenkinson Full of bitterness and hate, couldn't face his responsibilities. Mind you, he had a useless lump of ten-year-old boy at home. People round here said that lad never looked his dad in the face in his entire life. His head were always in a book or his ear were jammed up against radio or summat.

Henry You're talking to him, Mrs Jenkinson.

Mrs Jenkinson I know. Ezra Pratt were the biggest bore this side of Penistone Colliery. My husband banned him from this pub for going on and on about t'war. Then he cowardly hung hissen from a hook in the outside privvie.

Henry Mrs Jenkinson, you're a poisonous, lying —— !

Mrs Jenkinson I should watch out, if I were you! It's in the face. Parrot strangling, hangings, murders!

Henry Murder?

Mrs Jenkinson Don't tha know? My Cecil says it were all hushed up. That nightclub in Fish Hill. That club were deliberately burned to the ground wi'Teddy Braithwaite inside it!

Henry My Uncle Teddy was murdered?

Ben Am I playing on me tod or what?

Tommy By the heck! It's right nice of thee, Anna, but manager says it's lethal to me lethal left foot.

Councillor Lewthwaite enters. He wears a hearing aid

Cllr Lewthwaite Pint.

Mrs Jenkinson Coming up, Councillor Lewthwaite.

Cllr Lewthwaite (*adjusting his hearing aid*) Tha what? Didn't catch it. Have you seen Mr Hathersage, tonight. Mrs Jenkinson?

Henry Fred-unscrupulous-property-developer-Hathersage!

Mrs Jenkinson The Rolls isn't outside, is it? Well, Fred Hathersage isn't here.

Henry (*to Councillor Lewthwaite*) Good-evening, Councillor. I wonder if I could beg two favours. I met your daughter on holiday, could you ask her to get in touch? And would you be interested in being interviewed for my series "Proud Sons Of Thurmarsh"?

Cllr Lewthwaite Tha what? Didn't catch it.

Henry (*shouting*) I'm a journalist and I'd like to ask you a few important questions, Councillor.

The Lights cross-fade to:

SCENE 5

Outside the summerhouse in the Lewthwaites' garden on the freezing cold New Year's Eve of 1956 to '57

Popular music and radio news extracts play as the scene changes

Snow and moonlight. Light spills on stage from the offstage house. Sounds of a small party can be heard in the distance

Barry Frost, Fred Hathersage and Councillor Lewthwaite together, talking. They have cigars and drinks and wear overcoats. Their shadows are sinister on the grass

Henry enters, wrapped against the elements

The other three look embarrassed

Barry It's the reporter! Anyone for another drink?

Fred Hey up, Barry Frost, tha name'll get in't papers!

Cllr Lewthwaite He's playing the lead in *No, No, Nanette* and it's a closely guarded secret.

Fred Nay, Councillor, he used to lived in same lodgings wi'him.

Cllr Lewthwaite Oh ay, smelt o'cabbage and wet washing, so he said.

Fred He is a town hall plannin' officer when all is said and done. Am I right,
  Barry?
Barry Thank you, Fred.

  Barry Frost exits

Cllr Lewthwaite His wife's come back from Walsall but he's been dallying
  wi'a bit of fluff from t'newspaper, and this chap knows.
Fred Oh what a tangled web! (*Then to Henry*) Anything tha wants to know,
  I'm your man.
Henry Oh yes? What time is it, Mr Hathersage?
Fred No comment.

  Fred exits

Henry Aren't you going to congratulate me? I win the Nobel Prize for
  naïvety.
Cllr Lewthwaite Didn't catch it.

  *Sam Lewthwaite, an adolescent, enters. He charges about, singing
  mockingly*

Sam (*singing*) "Should old acquaintance be forgot and never brought ... la,
  la, la ... Should old acquaintance ..."
Cllr Lewthwaite It's nearly midnight, Sam!

  Councillor Lewthwaite exits

Sam (*to Henry*) Are you my sister's new lover?
Henry Shove off, object.

  Hilary enters, wrapped against the elements

Hilary Sam!
Sam What is it, Hilary?
Hilary It's rude to ignore the guests.
Sam Are you two going to have sexual intercourse?
Hilary Belt up, monster. (*To Henry*) Back soon, Henry, I'm on mince-pie
  duty.

  Hilary exits

Sam Our summerhouse is full of splinters.

Councillor Lewthwaite enters

Cllr Lewthwaite (*to Sam*) I've told you. (*To Henry*) My wife wants us all
    in.
Sam He'll get frostbite on his dick.
Cllr Lewthwaite (*adjusting his hearing aid*) Didn't catch it.
Henry The burning of the Cap Ferrat Nightclub could have been arson. The
    death of my uncle could have been murder. It's taken me a while to piece
    it altogether, and of course I've got no evidence but it's all a bit of
    coincidence, isn't it? His club was right in the middle of Fish Hill. Barry
    Frost got them to close the Temperance Hall, Haddock Road. And was it
    coincidental that a bloody great lorry drove into the middle of the Old
    Apothecary's Shop, the only listed building on Fish Hill? You're bulldoz-
    ing Paradise Lane for a city of glass.
Cllr Lewthwaite I know nothing about arson, murder or lorries.
Henry Anthony Eden denied collusion with France and Israel.
Cllr Lewthwaite The bottom's fallen out of drapery. My wife's ill. You're
    right, there is a development plan, a good plan. I've taken the odd back-
    hander, turned a blind eye, eased the occasional demolition order through
    committee. Nothing more.

Hilary enters

Hilary Dad, you're needed.
Cllr Lewthwaite A new year, Hilary. It'll have to be a good one.

Councillor Lewthwaite exits

Henry You're cold.
Hilary Not really. More frightened.
Henry Have you heard from Anna?
Hilary I had a dreary letter from Toulouse. She's staying with a pen-friend
    who's keen on mountaineering. Well, that's the official story. Actually,
    she's met this much older man, and she's living with him over there.
Henry I can't believe I made such a mistake in Italy.
Hilary Don't worry, it hasn't given me a superiority complex.
Henry I want to make love to you.
Hilary I bet you wish you'd gone to the New Year's Eve party at the
    newspaper offices.
Henry No, I don't.
Hilary Yes, you do. There isn't anyone here under forty except my horrible
    brother.
Henry Fred Hathersage was another of my "Proud Sons of Thurmarsh".

Hilary Daddy liked the one you wrote about him.
Henry I'm learning my editor's style.
Hilary Can't you write what you want?
Henry No. I'm burdened with terrific inexperience of the world, Hilary.
Hilary We'll both learn.

Sam enters, charging around

Sam You're going to miss it, you two, Mum says. Have you had it off yet?
    If so where have you put it?

Sam exits

Hilary (*calling after Sam*) You're a vile, mixed-up juvenile delinquent! (*To
    Henry*) He likes me to be rude to him. It's the only kind of affection he can
    deal with at the moment.
Henry Anna said you were mentally ill.
Hilary I've had a lot of depression. And I tried to kill myself. And I went very
    inward. If that's mental illness then …

Big Ben starts to chime in 1957

Hilary My parents taught me how to care, and now I can't stop. You know:
    people imprisoned without trial, the knock on the door in the middle of the
    night, the screams of the wounded in obscure border wars between
    countries whose names I can't pronounce. Every day I hear the screams of
    the world. (*Pause*) I love you. I'm in love with you.
Henry What a responsibility.

They kiss

*Big Ben sounds the first stroke of midnight. Snow falls in the moonlight.
"Auld Lang Syne" swells up*

The Lights cross-fade to:

SCENE 6

The bedroom of Henry's cramped flat in Fish Hill

Popular music and radio news extracts play as the scene changes

Henry is ill in bed with flu. Ginny stands nearby

Henry Are you sure you haven't got flu?

Ginny No. You've got flu, I just got a bad cold.

Henry We're both off sick. I think you should be in bed and I should be nursing you.

Ginny Don't be silly. (*She sneezes violently and has to lean on something for support*)

Henry (*too preoccupied to notice*) University must be an amazing experience.

Ginny gives Henry some medicine

Ginny Oh, you got another letter. (*She produces a letter from her pocket and hands it to Henry*)

Henry Oh Ginny, how could you! (*He tears it open and reads*)

Ginny I was too busy making you hot lemon. What can you find to write to each other?

Henry I'm racked with jealousy. All those intellectual types with beards. Having a girlfriend is agony.

Ginny Oh yeah. (*She practically passes out*)

Henry doesn't notice

Henry I'm terribly worried. *Take It from Here* did nothing to soothe my fevered brain. Ginny!

Ginny (*waking up*) Aagh! Sorry, I'll get your medicine.

Henry Ginny, what would you do if you knew something terrible, or even suspected something terrible, I mean terribly terrible, I mean so awful it would ruin a person's life, something so devastating ——

Ginny Is there an end to this sentence?

Henry And you were in love with his daughter?

Ginny It would depend.

Henry But what about an uncompromising commitment to the truth? The evils of society, of whatever kind, social, political, moral, although deeply intractable, have only one hope of amelioration, Ginny — constant statement of the truth.

Ginny I prefer *The Glums*, Henry.

Hilda (*off*) Henry!

Ginny ⎱ (*together*) Cousin Hilda!
Henry ⎰

Hilda I'm comin' in.

Henry and Ginny tidy up frantically

Ginny I'll go upstairs and lie down.

Henry Barry isn't coming round, is he?

Ginny exits

Hilda enters with shopping, including bananas

Hilda I thought tha might need cheerin' up. I'll get tha tea. I suppose tha's above and beyond meat faggots and peas now tha's a journalist.

Henry Very much the reverse. How are the gentlemen lodgers?

Hilda Mr Pettifer's had a bit of a comedown. He's been moved sideways off the cheese counter.

Henry Oh dear.

Hilda I had a Mr Brentwood for a few days but there were — hygiene problems. "Mr Brentwood," I said, "I've had complaints." "Complaints?" he said. "Complaints, that you smell." "Smell? Where?" he said. "In my basement," I said. "No, I mean where on me do I smell?" he said. I haven't been so embarrassed since you had your little problem when tha were little wi'tha little ...

Henry Backside.

Hilda Precisely. "All over," I said, "I believe the technical term is B.O." Then he said something very unnecessary.

Henry What?

Hilda He said, "I suppose you're telling me that B.O. stands for ... " I can't say it.

Henry Bugger off.

Hilda Precisely. "Mr Brentwood!" I said, "Only one person has ever spoken to me like that in my life, and that were a parrot."

Henry Cousin Hilda?

Hilda Ay?

Henry I'm engaged to be married. Her name's Hilary.

Hilda Ee. Well. Engaged! Well. And I've never even met her. Well. Mrs Wedderburn will be pleased.

Colin (*off*) Anyone home? Hallo!

Henry Colin?

Colin Edgeley enters with bananas

Colin Watcha, kid! (*He sees Hilda*) Ugh!

Henry Colin, if I wasn't at death's door I'd kill you!

Hilda Well, I just hope kitchen's hygienic.

Hilda exits

Ginny enters with bananas

Colin God, you look awful, Ginny.

Ginny That's just what I needed, Colin. I didn't want these, Henry.

Colin Can't stop. Urgent news. A big film company is coming to Thurmarsh.

Henry Thank you for the bananas, Ginny, Colin … (*he calls off*) Cousin Hilda.

Colin Does flu make you deaf? Films. The pictures. Film stars.

Henry I heard but I did not understand, Colin. Is the Thurmarsh underground deeply implicated?

Colin How did you know? (*To Ginny*) How did he know?

Ginny Oh Colin. D'you want some Lucozade?

Colin No. Angela Groyne has landed a leading part.

Ginny Why have you come to Henry to tell him that Angela Groyne's going to be in a film?

Colin Why else, kiddo? To save his career.

Ginny Henry!

Henry Mr Redrobe is going to sack me.

Ginny He's just made you "Uncle Jason".

Henry Only because he promoted Ted. I was summoned to his office after I reviewed that art exhibition for Denzil.

Ginny You wrote a very nice piece of pretentious rubbish.

Henry I know. But I didn't notice all the pictures had been hung upside down.

Colin Above, beyond and besides that, he's been lying his head off about some mysterious big story … .

Henry Unfortunately I'm unable to supply Mr Redrobe with the details of my big story. You wouldn't understand. It's a moral dilemma, Colin.

Colin Last time I bring you bananas and a friendly tip. Anyway, the film company needed a particular location. A grimy, wretched, dying earth overhung by a noxious angry sky — it's a science fiction film set in outer space — a no-man's land full of dust, swirling fog, and poisonous gases. They're shooting it at the bottom of Paradise Lane.

Henry In Fish Hill where I was born?

Colin Exactly. Is it a good story?

Henry Thanks, Colin.

Colin At least it's a step up from, "Girl, Seven, Lost Six Teeth In One Go." Oh, is anything else up in your neck of the woods?

Henry What d'you mean? What does he mean, Ginny?

Ginny What d'you mean, Colin?

Colin Nothing. Only Bill Holliday mentioned your name.

Henry Bill Holliday!

Colin Bill Holliday. Bill Holliday don't mention somebody's name without it meaning something.

Ginny What does it mean?

Colin I don't know. But it must mean something. Take care, kid. A few sharpened coins, remember.

Colin exits

Henry dives under the bedclothes

Henry Aagh! I'm dead! Somebody knows I know something.
Ginny What's the matter? What do you know?
Henry I don't know.
Ginny I'll get you some tea,
Henry I don't want tea. I want help. Help!
Ginny Don't be silly. Are you delirious?
Henry Somebody's going to kill me because I know too much!
Ginny What do you know?
Henry Everything! This proves it. Yesterday, on my way home, at the bus-stop, a car swerved towards me. It was deliberate, I saw the look in the driver's eye.
Ginny You are delirious.

Ginny starts to go, sneezing

Henry Ginny. If Barry does come round, any chance of keeping the noise down, or varying the operetta?
Ginny He's back with his wife. They've compromised. She's joining the Rawlaston Amateur Operatic. They are taking the joint leads in *No, No, Nanette*. Being artistic, he had to have an outlet for his animal lusts. Me.
Henry Ginny, Ginny, I wish you'd met a nice man. You deserve one.
Ginny Are you out of the running?
Henry I thought you knew. If I live, Hilary and I are engaged to be married.
Ginny I hope you'll both be very happy.

Ginny runs out of the room. As she goes, Hilda enters with a tray of food

Helen Cousin Hilda, could you look at my face? Can you see any doom in my eyes?
Hilda Never mind doom, eat your faggots while they're hot.

Henry stands up in bed suddenly. Hilda drops the tray of food to the ground and screams

Henry Aagh! Mrs Jenkinson was right, I've inherited the fate of a parrot-strangler!

The Lights cross-fade to:

SCENE 7

The Fish Hill area, round the corner from the burnt-out "Cap Ferrat"

Popular music and radio news extracts play as the scene changes

Henry is writing in a notebook

Henry "One of the few warehouses still in operation in the Fish Hill area is Bosomworths' General and Medical Stores. Today, amidst the incongruous trappings of a film company, a crane could still be seen hoisting goods into its cavernous loading bay — but for how much longer."

Neil Mallet enters, also with a notebook

Neil Nothing like it, is there? Hollywood.
Henry That's the Rundle Canal.
Neil Not if you've any imagination.
Henry Me and me mates used to race dried-up dog-turds off of the bridge. I were born right there. 23 Paradise Lane. Where they've parked the catering van. Hey, what are you doing here anyway, Neil Mallet? This is my story.
Neil Henry Pratt only writes about odd socks rediscovered in the garage.

Angela Groyne, in picturesque tatters, and Bill Holliday enter

Henry It's him!
Neil It's her!

Henry hides. Neil seizes the opportunity

Neil Excuse me, the *Argus*. Miss Groyne?
Angela Oh, the papers!
Bill I'm Miss Angela Groyne's manager, Bill Holliday.
Neil I understand Miss Groyne has a leading role in the film?
Angela Well, more supporting.
Bill She plays a corpse.
Angela The film is mainly corpses, really. There's this deadly gas or summat, so nobody can go out, but I was out already so I'm dead.
Bill Two bloody great monsters turn her over and examine her. First monster says, "Hey up, she's copped it," or words to that effect. Second monster

says, "Aye, and it's a right shame an' all because she looked a right tasty piece and that", or words to that effect.

Angela The monster comes from some strange planet or summat, and they all 'ave these incredible powers, like they can jump across t'Rundle.

Bill They've built this special spring. They've tried it four times. Landed in t'canal each time.

Angela You might think it's dead easy just to lie there dead, but it's not, it's dead difficult. You have to be right careful not to breathe in or out or owt.

Director (*off*) Miss Groyne, Angela darling. Where's the bloody corpse, for God's sake?

Angela Oops. I'm ready. I'm all ready.

Angela exits followed by Bill and Neil

Bill Hold your breath, like I showed you, Angie. And don't let them put your whole face in the muck.

Voices can be heard off, saying "OK luvvies, let's try it again" — that sort of thing

Doreen Frost enters, glacial

Henry I know you.

Doreen I would remember.

Henry What are you doing here?

Doreen What's it to you, droopy drawers?

Henry You're married to a man who used to lodge at the house where I used to live.

Doreen You are obviously not mentally defective, why are you pretending?

Henry I'm not, Mrs Frost, I'm tactfully trying to say I'm investigating your husband.

Doreen Who hired you? I knew it! He's got a second family! The two-timing bastard. And I agreed to sing soprano for him.

Henry No, no, I'm a newspaper reporter.

Doreen The gossip columns! Please don't hound me. Not for my sake, for my mother in Walsall.

Henry No, it's about compulsory purchase orders.

Doreen He's been buying things from catalogues again! Why did I marry him? Whatever made me fall for an amateur tenor who likes dressing in women's underwear?

Henry Does he? Ginny kept that quiet.

Doreen Who's Ginny?

Henry Never heard of her.

Doreen Who are you? Why can't you leave me alone?

Henry What were you doing in George Timpley's? Timpley and Nephews. The tobacconist. Just now.

Doreen I bought twenty Craven A. Is this something you'll put in the papers?

Henry What's your opinion of the fact that despite having miraculously escaped devastation in the recent fire Timpley and Nephews has been condemned?

Doreen Not by me, I'm not censorious by nature.

Henry No, by the Council Planning Office. Well, it's not actually condemned yet. George Timpley has informed me that they've offered to buy it.

Doreen Why?

Henry So they can knock it down. Mrs Frost, if George Timpley doesn't sell, your husband will make a demolition order on the grounds that it's unsafe. All the neighbouring properties are in the same position. Getting a sizable rake-off, our Barry, hey?

Doreen I see your game. You're pretending to be an obnoxious little worm but really you're insinuating yourself in to my good offices so I'll say something to incriminate Barry. Well, you'll have to try some other Council employee's wife or fancy woman because my lips are sealed.

Doreen exits

Bill enters

Bill I know you.

Henry No, you don't.

Bill I do and I want a word.

Henry Do you?

Bill I've a message from someone quite important.

Henry I don't know anything. For certain, that is.

Bill Which philosopher is that then? Hegel? Nietzshe? Much as I would like to indulge in a bit of intellectual one-up-manship I've got to get back to keep an eye on the talent. My friend, my good friend, Cecil E. Jenkinson, doesn't want you in his pub.

Henry The *Navigation*? My dad's old pub?

Bill He says you're bad memories. And he don't want bad memories.

Henry Was that all, Mr Holliday?

Bill Bill, please.

Bill exits

Neil enters

Neil This is it, Henry Pratt. I've had it up to here.

Henry Neil, a confrontation will merely cause things to be said that can never be unsaid.

Neil Give up, you haven't got what it takes to be a journalist and never will. I knew from your first day.

Henry Don't resent me because of your own inadequacies. Anybody would appear popular compared to you. Are you jealous of me or something? Was it Helen?

Neil Our great and good editor has got your number. You are as good as sacked.

Henry Something has just clicked. Why didn't I think of it before? You've got a brother in the print room!

Neil Jeremy. So what?

Henry I see your game. You deliberately arranged all those misprints to sabotage my career.

Neil My lips are sealed.

A large crate on a crane hook falls from the sky, landing on Neil Mallet

Henry Someone has just tried to murder me and got the wrong man. Or the implacable hand of fate has just killed Neil Mallet with a crate of surgical trusses.

Henry tends to the body

A monster with a huge green head and tentacles enters. The monster stares at Henry, waves good-naturedly, then removes its head to reveal Arnold Nutley

I know you.

Arnold Beats working. I don't in fact mean that, it is actually a highly-skilled occupation but you've got to say something when you take the head off. Problem?

Henry He's dead.

Arnold No, people would be shouting and making a fuss. He's probably stunned. Let me have a look.

Henry Are you St John's Ambulance as well?

Arnold No. You looked pretty useless, that's all.

Henry I'm from the *Argus*.

Arnold I've always wanted to do "Proud Sons of Thurmarsh".

Director (*off*) Stunts!

Arnold What do I think of Suez? Well, I don't know much about it really. I just think we've split the nation, weakened the Commonwealth, the

Atlantic Alliance and the United Nations, diverted the world's attention from the Russian atrocities in Hungary, and harmed forever our capacity to take a credible position of moral leadership in the world. But that's only my opinion. He's alive.

Director (*off*) Stunts! Where is that Nutley fellow?

Henry Of course! You are Arnold "Tree-Trunk" Nutley. Who paid you?

Director (*louder, more peremptory; off*) Stunts!

Arnold My art calls. Prove it. I've never driven a lorry. I can't even say "apothecary".

Henry Then how did you know what I was talking about?

Director (*off*) Is there a professional on this location or am I a Martian?

Arnold Get help, he could be concussed.

Arnold exits

Director (*off*) OK, we're going for a take. Absolute quiet, everybody. Three, three, seven, take five. Action.

We hear the sounds of a contraption working, then a splash

Bugger!

Neil Bugger!

The Lights cross-fade to:

SCENE 8

A pretty street café in Cap Ferrat on the Côte D'Azur seaside

Popular music and radio news extracts play as the scene changes

Anna sits at a table on which are two cups of coffee. She is wearing expensive jewellery and has bags of shopping with her. Henry sits at another table looking at a photograph

A French waiter enters

Anna explains in careful French that her companion has gone to the toilet but they would like more coffee when he returns

Waiter (*French accent*) Two more coffees when he gets back, righto love.

Anna Thank you.

Henry Ah, you're English. Anna!

Anna Henry!

Henry Anna! I was just looking at a photograph of Hilary.

Anna Congratulations on your engagement. I had a letter. On holiday?

Henry Not really. I'm here with relations. I had a big problem to sort out, my career's going through a sticky patch.

Anna What better place than Cap Ferrat for a socialist with problems.

Henry Ah, oh yes. I've been privileged with a lot of suffering. Anna.

Anna It takes all sorts.

Henry I know I sound pompous but I've been humiliated with the best of them.

Anna I think we should be making innocuous entertaining chit-chat, Henry.

Henry I've come up with a major scandal. You remember my Uncle Teddy who died in the fire?

Anna Vaguely.

Henry Well he might have been murdered; but even worse than that, Hilary's father is involved, he's been taking large bribes. I've been agonizing over whether to keep quiet for Hilary's sake.

Anna Where are your relations?

Henry My Auntie Doris is ——

Anna Your Auntie Doris is here!

Henry Yes, she's gone shopping for sea-bass. My late Uncle Teddy loved sea-bass and Geoffrey Porringer, her new husband, has gone for a stroll because she keeps talking about how much my late Uncle Teddy loved sea-bass.

Anna Do you like surprises, Henry? (*She indicates off stage*)

Henry looks

Henry My God!

Teddy (*off*) Trust bloody you to run me to earth!

Henry Uncle Teddy!

Teddy enters in holiday clothes

Teddy Hallo, Henry.

Henry You aren't dead?

Teddy This isn't just luck, is it? Oh hell-fire, it is, isn't it? You've bumped into us by accident?

The Waiter enters, bringing the coffee

Henry I'm here with Auntie Doris and Geoffrey Porringer.

Teddy What ! Anna, come on. (*He moves to leave*)

Henry They're on the other side of town.

Teddy How insensitive of them to come here with me dead.

Henry You aren't dead.

Teddy They don't know that. (*To the Waiter*) Champagne. We'll celebrate.
You've met Mrs Wedderburn, have you? My naughty sense of humour.
You remember Cousin Hilda's best friend? Alice Wedderburn was the first
girl I ever did it with, behind the tramsheds. She was Alice Crapper then.

Anna I drew the line at Mr and Mrs Crapper.

Henry A body was found in your nightclub. A man was murdered so that
you could live in the south of France with a younger woman!

Teddy Anna, see you back at the villa. Can you sneak off and join us for
dinner, Henry? We're having sea-bass.

Anna exits

The wind can be heard, rising

The Waiter brings champagne

Henry I'm glad you're aren't dead. I'm very glad.

Teddy Henry, you were never supposed to get fond of me.

There is a slight pause

Henry Have you remembered I'm a journalist, Uncle Teddy?

Teddy Oh. Nobody was murdered.

Henry Who was it?

Teddy Who?

Henry The body in the *Cap Ferrat* nightclub.

Teddy The headmaster of the Thurmarsh Grammar School. We were about
the same size,

Henry You murdered Mr E. F. Crowther?

Teddy He died of natural causes. Henry, don't get excited, there are Germans
and Dutch and Danes here.

Henry I did an article on him, the "Proud Sons of Thurmarsh" series — and
I've sat in many an assembly presided over by him. How?

Teddy He died of a heart attack. In an exotic brothel run by Derek Parsonage,
in Thurmarsh. While strung up by a rope from the ceiling. Entirely encased
in chain-mail.

Henry You call that natural causes?

Teddy It was natural to him. It's not as uncommon a type of thing as a you
might think.

Henry He lectured us on moral values.

Teddy Hypocrisy is not as uncommon as you might think. We hushed it up and used his remains. Of course his family think he just walked out on them; I hope they would prefer that to the truth, don't you?

Henry What a story, what a story!

Teddy More champagne?

Henry Thank you. Derek got the insurance for you, did he? Plus the bribes from the developers for burning it down.

The Lights dim during the following; lights come on along the promenade

I'm sorry, Teddy. Of course you're hurt because someone you treated as a son is going to expose you. Hilary, my fiancée …

Teddy Congratulations; Anna told me.

Henry She will have to face the truth about her father, same as I'm facing the truth about you. Rangoon here you come.

Teddy I hope you are not enjoying this.

Henry I've never been through anything more horrible in my life.

Teddy You realize, of course, that I shall have to murder you.

Henry Oh my God! I never thought of that. I felt threatened in Thurmarsh but I thought I was safe here.

Teddy It will be an act of pure generosity on my part. People have to be protected from you.

Henry From me?

Teddy Yes.

Henry Who?

Teddy The world at large.

Henry What?

Teddy If you lived they'd all be bored to death.

Henry You can't murder me because I'm not a scintillating personality.

Teddy I'm exaggerating, it's just a few dozen I need to protect from you.

Henry The champagne! It's poisoned!

Teddy As if I'd ruin good bubbly. You never could stand being teased. Why should I resort to violence? You won't publish. In fact you won't tell anyone you've met me, except perhaps Hilary.

Henry I will publish. I've got principles, unlike you.

Teddy Do you need me to spell it out? Just how many lives do you want to ruin? The dead headmaster's family, the Lewthwaites, Fred Hathersage, the Frosts, Hilda, Doris. How is she going to feel knowing I've been here all the time living with a younger woman? Think about it. Think hard.

There is a slight pause

Henry You're a bastard.

Teddy There are much worse around than your Uncle Teddy. Now stop
being so big-headed and come and have dinner. We're having sea-bass.

The stars come out over Cap Ferrat, the "Dambusters' March" swells up

   Hilary appears, a vision

Confetti falls

THE END

FURNITURE AND PROPERTY LIST

ACT I

SCENE 1

Off stage: Suitcase (**Henry**)
Luggage (**Doreen**)

Personal: **Henry**: notebook and pen

SCENE 2

On stage: Desks with typewriters and phones

SCENE 3

On stage: Pub tables and chairs
Drinks for **Ginny** and **Henry**
Copy of the *Evening Argus*

Off stage: Drink for **Henry** (**Denzil**)
Drink for **Henry** (**Ted**)

SCENE 4

On stage: Living-room furniture
Small television

Off stage: Mug (**Norman**)

Personal: **Henry**: copy of the *Evening Argus*

SCENE 5

On stage: Editor's desk. *On it*: letters
Office chairs

SCENE 6

On stage: Counter
              Café tables and chairs
              Coffee cups and saucers etc.

SCENE 7

On stage: Rugs for **Mr Hargreaves**, **Mrs Hargreaves**, **Diana Hargreaves**,
              Paul Hargreaves, **Lampo Davey** and **Henry**
              Vacuum flask
              Full picnic

SCENE 8

On stage: Parts of setting for *The Desert Song*; flats, braces, archway, treads
              made from beer crates and planks

Off stage: Pile of chorus dresses (**Roger**)
              Camel (**Roger**)
              Large, empty tea urn, packets of sugar, tea, tin of coffee, extension lead
              and adaptor plug (**Roger**)

SCENE 9

On stage: Bedsitting-room furniture
              Henry's coat

SCENE 10

On stage: Suggestion of half-prepared nightclub

SCENE 11

On stage: Small television
              Scrapbook for **Hilda**

SCENE 12

On stage: Completed nightclub with "traditional fake southern French décor"

Off stage: Copy of the *Evening Argus* (**Teddy**)

SCENE 13

Off stage: Labelled box (**Stage Management**)
                 Trick cigars, funny noses, sneezing powder, plastic fried eggs, farting
                     cushion (**Stage Management**)

Personal: **Henry**: notebook and pen

ACT II

SCENE 1

On stage: Lich-gate
                 Gravestones

Off stage: Pint of beer (**Eric Lugg**)

Personal: **Geoffrey**: watch
                 Fred: cigar
                 Henry: confetti, camera, notebook

SCENE 2

On stage: Tent walls
                 Two beds. *In one*: dummy with hidden rope tied around neck
                 Cigarettes for **Henry** and **Brian**

SCENE 3

On stage: Café tables and chairs
                 Coffee cups and saucers etc.

SCENE 4

On stage: Bar with optics, pumps etc.
                 Pub tables and chairs
                 Dart board
                 Darts

Off stage: Tray of drinks (**Tommy**)

Personal: **Henry**: notebook, pen
                 Councillor Lewthwaite: hearing aid (worn throughout)

SCENE 5

On stage: Summerhouse exterior

Off stage: Cigars and drinks (**Barry**, **Fred**, **Councillor Lewthwaite**)

SCENE 6

On stage: As ACT I SCENE 9

Off stage: Shopping, including bananas (**Hilda**)
                Bananas (**Colin**)
                Bananas (**Ginny**)
                Tray of food (**Ginny**)

Personal: **Ginny**: letter

SCENE 7

Off stage: Large crate on crane hook (in flies, on ropes/wires)

Personal: **Henry**: notebook, pen
                Neil: notebook, pen

SCENE 8

On stage: Café tables. *On one*: two cups of coffee
                Photograph for **Henry**

Off stage: Two cups of coffee (**Waiter**)
                Bottle of champagne and glasses (**Waiter**)

LIGHTING PLOT

Practical fittings required: none

ACT I

To open: Darkness

Cue 11   **Henry** rushes out   (Page 27)
             Cross-fade to general interior lighting;
             "Cap Ferrat" Nightclub

Cue 12   **Henry**: " … you could ever have her back?"   (Page 29)
             Cross-fade lights to general interior lighting; living-room

Cue 13   **Hilda** and **Mr O'Reilly** puzzle over the scrapbook   (Page 30)
             Cross-fade lights to general interior lighting;
             "Cap Ferrat" Nightclub

Cue 14   The *Côte D'Azur Cuties* falter   (Page 33)
             Cross-fade lights to general exterior night-time lighting;
             outside the "Cap Ferrat", with effect of flames roaring
             into the sky

Cue 15   Popular music and radio news extracts play   (Page 36)
             Black-out

ACT II

To open: Darkness

Cue 16   Organ music   (Page 37)
             Bring up lights on general exterior setting; church

Cue 17   **Henry**: "Oh, Lorna!"   (Page 42)
             Cross-fade to tent interior; "nightmare" setting

Cue 18   Rain sounds stop   (Page 43)
             Lighting indicates dawn breaking

Cue 19   **Brian** exits   (Page 44)
             Dim lights to night effect; "nightmare" setting

Cue 20   **Botney**: " … your next fifteen years!"   (Page 44)
             Cross-fade to general exterior lighting; Siena café

Cue 21   **Lampo** and **Denzil** shake hands; beat   (Page 47)
             Cross-fade to general interior lighting; pub

Cue 22   **Henry**: "… a few important questions, Councillor."   (Page 52)
             Cross-fade to moonlight effect on snow;
             light spill to indicate offstage house

Cue 23   *Auld Lang Syne* swells up   (Page 55)
             Cross-fade to general interior lighting; **Henry**'s *flat*

EFFECTS PLOT

ACT I

Cue 13   **Paul**: "… the playing fields of Dalton?"   (Page 20)
Whistle blows

Cue 14   Lights cross-fade to Temperance Hall   (Page 23)
Popular music and radio news extracts; fade.
Short burst of "The Desert Song" finale

Cue 15   Lights cross-fade to **Henry**'s flat   (Page 25)
Radio news extracts; fade to amateur tenor
singing "My Desert is Waiting" and energetic
bedspring sounds

Cue 16   **Doris**: "… see Teddy, will you Henry?"   (Page 27)
Scream of brakes and thunderous crash
as vehicle smashes into building

Cue 17   Lights cross-fade to "Cap Ferrat" Nightclub   (Page 27)
Popular music and radio news extracts; fade

Cue 18   Lights cross-fade to living-room   (Page 29)
Popular music and radio news extracts; fade

Cue 19   Lights cross-fade to "Cap Ferrat" Nightclub   (Page 30)
Popular music and radio news extracts; fade

Cue 20   When ready   (Page 30)
Teddy's *voice over speakers* (*live or recorded*)
— dialogue as p. 30

Cue 21   **Teddy**: "… Boycott and his Northern Serenaders!"   (Page 30)
Band plays slightly naughty dance tune slightly naughtily

Cue 22   **Colin** exits   (Page 33)
Teddy's *voice over speakers* (*live or recorded*)
— dialogue as p. 33

Cue 23   **Teddy**: " … the *Côte D'Azur Cuties*!"   (Page 33)
Music for "Côte D'Azur Cuties"

Cue 24   Lights cross-fade to exterior of "Cap Ferrat"   (Page 34)
Popular music and radio news extracts;
fade into sounds of fire engines, crowds, ladders, fire-hoses
— continue under scene

Cue 25   **Timpley**: "Fifty-seven. Oh, my God. Why?"   (Page 35)
Small explosion

Cue 26   **Colin**: "Bill Holliday's revenge."   (Page 36)
               Ominous creaks

Cue 27   **Derek**: "There goes the joke shop!"   (Page 36)
               Explosion

Cue 28   All stare off in the light of the fire   (Page 36)
               Popular music and radio news extracts

ACT II

Cue 29   When ready   (Page 37)
               Popular music and radio news extracts; fade,
               *   then bring up sound of enthusiastic organ playing,*
               *   with lots of mistakes*

Cue 30   All exit   (Page 39)
               Wedding music plays, full of wonder and inaccuracies

Cue 31   Lights cross-fade to tent interior   (Page 42)
               Popular music and radio news extracts; fade to rain effect

Cue 32   **Henry** and **Brian** laugh   (Page 43)
               Hundreds of squaddies laugh

Cue 33   **Body**, **Botney** and **Brian** vanish   (Page 43)
               Fade rain sounds; bring up birdsong

Cue 34   **Henry** gets up   (Page 43)
               Officer'*s voice through megaphone* (*live or recorded*)
               *   — dialogue as p.43*

Cue 35   **Henry**: " ... compassionate grounds."   (Page 44)
               Officer'*s voice through megaphone* (*live or recorded*)
               *   — dialogue as p.44*

Cue 36   Night falls   (Page 44)
               Rain effect

Cue 37   Lights cross-fade to café exterior   (Page 45)
               Popular music and radio news extracts; fade

Cue 38   Lights cross-fade to pub interior   (Page 48)
               Cut rain effect; popular music and radio news extracts; fade

Cue 39   Lights cross-fade to summerhouse exterior   (Page 52)
               Popular music and radio news extracts;
               *   fade to distant sounds of party*

Cue 40	**Hilary**: " If that's mental illness then …" *Opening chimes of Big Ben midnight peal*	(Page 55)
Cue 41	First stroke of midnight peal *Snow effect; "Auld Lang Syne" plays*	(Page 55)
Cue 42	Lights cross-fade to **Henry**'s flat *Popular music and radio news extracts; fade*	(Page 55)
Cue 43	Lights cross-fade to Fish Hill area *Popular music and radio news extracts; fade*	(Page 60)
Cue 44	**Director**: " …take five. Action." *Sounds of contraption, then splash*	(Page 64)
Cue 45	Lights cross-fade to café in Cap Ferrat *Popular music and radio news extracts; fade*	(Page 64)
Cue 46	**Anna** exits *Wind rises*	(Page 66)
Cue 47	Stars come out *"Dambusters" march*	(Page 68)
Cue 48	**Hilary** appears *Confetti*	(Page 68)